THE ESSENTIAL PIANO TEACHER'S GUIDE

The Sheli Nan Method by Sheli Nan

With ease of use in mind, "The Essential Piano Teacher's Guide" imparts a message about the joy that results from teaching and performing music while seeking to inspire and stimulate the creativity of the instructor as well as the student. Emphasizing the idea of community, this book utilizes the great teachings from the baroque period to the exciting rhythms of Afro-cuban percussion. It is a plan for the modern music teacher looking for a multi-cultural multi-ethnic approach to teaching learning enjoying and performing piano today.

PLUS: THE RHYTHMTWISTERS PROGRAM

Tech-Clazz Publishing Company
Berkeley, California

Tech-Clazz Publishing Compnay
P.O. Box 5173
Berkeley, California 94705
e-mail: TheMuse23@aol.com
world wide web: http://www.shelinan.com

Printed in the United States of America

Cover and book design by Elizabeth Azen
e-mail: azen@usa.net
Instrument illustrations by Rob Sato

ISBN 0-9700830-0-9

ABOUT THE AUTHOR

Pianist, harpsichordist, percussionist, composer, author and teacher, Sheli Nan, has resided in the Bay Area for over twenty years. "The Music Studio", her teaching studio, has served as the laboratory for the evolution of her musical ideas. She has developed a method of keyboard study utilizing the great teachings from the baroque period to the exciting rhythms of African percussion. Sheli has worked for the San Francisco Symphony AIM program and she has been on the roster for the YOUNG AUDIENCES Program. She has composed, recorded and performed classical and original music extensively on piano and harpsichord and she performed on keyboard and percussion in ensemble with The World Connection, a Nigerian band, for three years. Sheli has devoted her life to studying and teaching music and to training others.

TABLE OF CONTENTS

FORWARD

This book describes a unique approach to music instruction. It is a multi-cultural synthesis of the work I have done in my studio for the past 22 years. It is a method book for piano teachers that incorporates the baroque teachings of historically informed performance, and the percussion training from the African and Afro-Cuban traditions. It will stimulate the music teacher with its inherent possibilities for learning.

When I sat down to write this book I had a preconceived idea of how I would organize my thoughts. I originally devised the idea of developing the book in three different sections. The first was to be inspirational, the second was to be anecdotal, and the third was to be concrete lesson plans.

And yet, as I began to write, the movement of my hand took on a meaning all it's own. Much like when I sit down at the piano to improvise a composition, the words, like notes, begin to appear, each with their own rhythm and sound.

When I compose, different sections of the piece become apparent, not always in chronological order. Fragments or phrases that are meaningful, appear. Then they are joined by other musical moments linked not by chronology but by musical need.

I developed the book in much the same way. The ideas, so long in development in my studio, in my heart, in my soul mind and body clamored for the light of day. Like a composition, I have structured them into a formal framework. Now that I have released them into the world, I hope they will become your ideas as well as mine.

I dedicate this book to my husband Sam Tabachnik, my children Azriel, Maaseiah and Aviva, my parents Berta and Jack Hershcopf, and my in-laws Olga and Joe Tabachnik, my aunt Jennie Feinman and to my brilliant teachers; Laurette Goldberg, Vivian Rivkin, Wanda Krasoff, Carole Chilton, Carlos Federico, Suru Ekeh and Julian White. I thank all of my students past and present, all of the friends that have always supported me, and all those in the musical community and greater musical world everywhere. I want to acknowledge music teachers for doing the good work, the meaningful and thoughtful work, so often under appreciated by the general public. It is a labor of love and service. You are making a difference. Your generosity of spirit is what takes the next generation of people down the magnificent path to musical fluency.

A special note of recognition to Igor Kipnis, Gilbert Martinez, Adesoji Odukogbe, Brian Hand, Babatunde Olatunji, Sandra Brod and Bennett Markel.

With love,

Sheli Nan

INTRODUCTION

Music is a language. We speak this language and listen to it. We experience the language of music at our instruments. We experience the language of music when we listen to one another perform. And we speak the language of music when we discuss all of the various aspects of our musical world.

All sound that is created never really goes away. The sound travels beyond our ability to hear it anymore, much like when we throw a rock into a pond. We watch in fascination as the ripples made by the rock grow larger and larger. Such is the experience of sound. The sound we create continues to expand forever outward. This ability we have, to add to the great harmony around us, conscious of it or not, affects us as we create our moments of beauteous sound. The Muse calls to us. We hear our pieces in our minds. We feel like we are being taught celestially, supported by a great and never ending tradition. We become part of a cosmic movement full of beauty and the deep rich struggle to be worthy of this spiritual heritage, linking us back to the beginning of our species.

The language of music is a deep heart-felt experience expressing itself through all of one's many facets. It is intensely physical. Our hands.We are so grateful for our hands. Our hands express our love - we hold one another and hug one another - we trace the outlines of one another's faces - a child explores her mother's features - a baby holds his toes, claps his hands, explores his world. What does a mother not do with her hands? She heals, she loves, she cooks, she cleans, she works. What man has not experienced the power of his personality when grasping the wheel of a car, building or fixing something, working with his hands, loving, healing, nurturing? Now put an instrument into those hands. Give baby her rattle. Give the kids drums. Give Mom a keyboard, give Dad a guitar. Whatever the instrument, our hands now eagerly explore the instrument we hold. Imagine our delight when we realize a moment of beauty, sound, that we have created, that belongs to us alone.

We take this experience a step further. We are pleased and gladdened by the sound we created so we try to repeat it. When we do, we rejoice.

The simple act of hitting two sticks together becomes an intricate maneuver when we learn a pattern. After we have improvised and enjoyed the physical feeling of holding those two sticks, after we have played them in all different positions, after we have gone from playing very quietly to hitting with all of our strength, after all that experimentation, improvisation, we settle into a pattern.

Which pattern do we naturally feel most comfortable with? I believe it is the pattern based on the beat of four. Perhaps it is because we have 2 hands and 2 legs, or 2 eyes and 2 ears. There is a comfort in the rhythmic pattern of four. The youngest child to the oldest adult can relate to it. So we begin with a pattern of 1-2-3-4. We begin to arrange the sound and our movements. And glory, when we are playing together in the studio, when we do it all at once, we not only are being called upon to coordinate our sound with an idea, but to coordinate our sound with one another. This takes intense listening.

LISTENING is a vital part of the musical experience.One cannot be a musician without actively consciously engaging in the act of listening. It makes no difference if there is technical progress. Without listening we are lost. To play music without listening is like being on a boat, lost at sea, forever rowing, never arriving. The act of listening is our covenant with the Muse. It is the way we pay obeisance or homage if you will. It is the gift we give back to the great force that has so generously given to us.

This act of listening is perhaps the most difficult of all the facets of musical training. We are called upon to replace the inner voices of critique with a clarity of attention when we play. This is a secret. It is this supreme act of concentration and will that gives us our most "at one" experiences musically. When we are steeped in our composition, improvisation, practice, rehearsal and performance, we have achieved a unity of design that brings us into focus. We no longer exist separately from the divine we give voice to.

Within my musical world, I strive to create a community. This is a community linked by a common bond, the language of music. My students range in age from 3 to 65. Men, women, and children of all ages comes to my studio to learn piano, harpsichord, voice, guitar, Afro-Cuban percussion and composition. They all grapple with the profound exhilarating and frustrating experience of expressing themselves within this language. But how to teach this?

My method gives people another path toward this profound experience. The process of becoming a musician is a process of *civilizing.* One cannot be part of a family, friendship, community without the very necessary skill of listening. Once we are able to listen, we are able to contextualize our own sounds. That is the first step toward becoming a human being that can utilize all of our senses in a maximum way.

COMMUNITY

When I think of the concept of community these thoughts come to mind. One is of a group of people who share the same interests and who speak the same language. A musical community, made up of varied ages of people, is just that. I am speaking now of my community of mentor, students and colleagues. All of us are engaged in the act of beauty. We are connecting with our creativity and we are feeling better about ourselves, more hopeful, even optimistic.

By struggling with the greatest human creations, like a piece by Johann Sebastian Bach - we reinvent our world. We may transcend ourselves and perceive the magnificent potential of our species. Hence our community - one imbued with the spirit of work and reward, both physical and metaphysical, holds us, by the tenets of our musical language, to a greater (more aspiring) version of ourselves which is constantly striving.

Now imagine the possibilities when we think about speaking this musical tongue to one another. And here I refer to the words of music. Imagine an older person sitting down with a younger person and playing for one another. Perhaps the younger person is holding the score while the older person is playing from another score. The conversation could go something like this:

"I think that F is sharped in the fourth measure."

"But in my edition there is an F natural."

"But are you using an urtext edition?" (see page 109.)

"Well, let's check it out. Anyway, how do you think it sounds with the F sharped, and then with the F not sharped?"

And on and on.

We immediately have new options to communicate with one another, options that transcend age. Engaged in our task of deciphering the minds hearts and souls of the Great Masters, (and in so doing the minds hearts and souls of ourselves) we come together to read share study and LISTEN!

Because my musical community ranges in age so greatly sometimes I teach the entire family! Although they each take private lessons with me, when at home people must schedule practice time. Parents feel pride and are encouraged by realizing that they are role models for their children by being engaged in a task (practicing) that requires discipline, that is hard, that does not give immediate satisfaction, and that shows them working toward a conclusion. Children are thrilled to be learning concurrently with their parents. An entire world of communication, deep rich meaningful and scholarly, is pursued by these lucky families.

With the teenager, when conversations frequently distill to the essential:

"Have you cleaned up your room? Taken out the garbage? Done your homework? Practiced?"

You can now add:

"I loved that Beethoven. Could you explain why you pedaled it that way? "

We have obviously raised the level of intelligible discourse. It is so interesting to talk music. If we, in our musical communities, go to a concert together, or listen to a CD, once again we can talk. We can talk style, era, instrumentation, interpretation, etc. The concept of viable musical community is one of practice and communication.

THE ART OF LEARNING MUSIC

Learning music is not linear. We are seduced into believing that it is a linear experience primarily because our educational system is organized as a linear process. This is the way we learn at school. We are given a number of facts. We then organize these facts coherently. After this we produce a result from the facts that have been learned.

Whether this result is a paper, a project, or some other tangible criteria, we now have a product that can be judged. Not only can this product be judged, but it can also be compared to someone else's product. We therefore create a time line for educational expectations that is based on arriving at a certain point with a certain result that can be quantified and qualified in regard to the products and the results of the peer group.

Although we can superimpose this structure on the learning of music, it is a mistake to believe that this model will deliver the product in the same way.

It is easy to think of music in a linear fashion. When we hold the musical blueprint in our hands, in other words, a piece of paper with dots on it that is commonly referred to as music, we read it in much the same way we read words. There are lines and spaces. The music follows lines, the notes have a graceful visual linear relationship to one another and the piece has a beginning and an ending. When we look at a keyboard we also see a pattern that emerges. We speak of going up the keyboard into the treble, and going down the keyboard into the bass. Our hands move up and down traversing the keyboard. We learn from our books, and certainly when the student is a beginner, there is a progression from easy material to more difficult material. The comparison ends there.

Although time is often a linear concept, particularly when we wear time on our wrists and refer back constantly to this arbitrary organization of our day, our heart beat gives us another sense of time. We have an internal organic relationship to our inner rhythm. For example, let us speak of the purely physical aspect of the experience first. Many people forget to breathe when they are playing piano. This happens particularly when a student comes to a difficult passage. The teaching and incorporation of breath is an essential aspect to the successful and coherent performance of music. As in any language, one needs to know when to pause, and when to continue with one's thought. The word breath, in Latin, has the same roots as the word *inspire.* To breathe in can also be conjured as inspiration. Here we have a profound concept. Breath is linked to creativity. When the student understands how breath works in concert with playing piano she has a new tool for supporting the difficult technique required.

Learning music is an all inclusive experience. It does not follow a path marked from A to Z.

Most of us have had the experience of practicing, listening to, or performing a piece of music that seems to last forever that in fact lasts for less than 5 minutes. Time is an abstract form that we shape to suit our needs. If we put the linear dimension of time on hold for a moment, musical time, rather than proceeding line wise, travels into a deep unfathomed spot that is not always quantifiable. I am not referring to the metronome* right now. I am referring to the experience of learning.

Although we time the lessons, the experience of learning does not go by the clock. It goes into the deep place the student holds dear. A good teacher strives to reach the vessel of creativity that each student carries within himself. In so doing, the process can take years. It is banal and unnecessary to compare one student's journey on a time line with another student's journey. Each person travels at his or her own unique pace.

This is the beauty of the process. The product is a delightful mingling of the hard earned technique, the vision and generosity of the composer, and the beauty of the language. The student's own feeling of accomplishment is coupled with all she has learned about herself from the process. And there is all the information that has been learned from the composer as well.

Along with breath there is appropriate posture, arm and wrist technique and finger placement. Because this organic process requires such attention to physical detail, there are no shortcuts. The path meanders as each new concept is introduced and refined. Some weeks a student might just work on his finger technique at the harpsichord*. After this a student might just work on trouble spot (see page 45) passages for a month.

Because the scope of the process is so grand, the work is about the many detailed musical steps that are taken to reach the greater outcome. How do the pieces fit together? An apt and marvelous example to use with your students is the analogy of the puzzle. A Bach fugue is like a puzzle. Depending on the complexity of the fugue, it can be like a 10,000 piece puzzle where all of the pieces are no more than a sixteenth of an inch. Imagine the work that goes into this. The process itself becomes the raison d'etre. Of course once the puzzle is finished, the picture will be admired by all. It is in the learning of all the separate pieces though, that the validity of the process and the wealth of information occurs.

The most gifted teacher will take the endless task of learning music and make each achievement significant for the student. Every level on the musical pathway is one of inspiration and meaning.

It is said that there will always be a teacher that can teach a student something. This means that no matter how advanced one gets, there will always be someone to share something new, or contextualize a musical idea somewhat differently. The process seen in this light gives the learning a more circular dimension. One is never ever finished in the musical world. There is no graduation per se. It is impossible to learn all there is to know. The most advanced pianist in the world will discover something new with the very same material that he has performed any number of times. He may discover a new piece of information from the Master he is playing, or he may

*see glossary

overhear a comment about the piece that allows him to hear and experience the piece in a new way.

Because of the elasticity of the learning, there is always room for more information. It becomes a blessing that the student never has to cease being a student at any age or level. The greater the musician, the more he or she knows, the greater the understanding that there is so much more that he or she will never know.

Although this can be a daunting thought at first, it becomes a great comfort. How marvelous to be involved in a heritage of musical literature that has boundaries that are constantly expanding. One brings one's own unique voice to the tapestry of the conversation. This removes the need for peer judgment and peer pressure. Each student learns at his or her own pace and IT IS OKAY. To falsely superimpose a learning schedule, following the linear model, does a great disservice to the student and to the process.

The art of learning music travels a profound route that goes in many different physical and spiritual directions. The intellectual stimulation coupled with the original voice of the student, provides a mental support system for the great conversations taking place in the human politic. Against the backdrop of this technique the student is given access to some of the greatest creations the human species has produced. This depth and enrichment becomes a lifelong quest for the student's essential voice. The teacher lucky enough to provide the tools for this journey will be privy to the most wonderful moments of discovery, joy and intimacy that the teaching experience offers.

TEACHING ESSENTIALS

TEACHER'S ATTITUDE

It is important to consider oneself a strict teacher. There is musical information that must be imparted to the student, and the student must learn to be a competent pianist. Because this is an oral tradition, there is an orderly progression to the material taught. It is important to be thorough.The manner though, in which the student is taught, is not strict. It is kind, respectful and serious, with room for personality, a sense of humor, and the serious fun of learning and creating.

The appropriate attitude for the piano teacher is one of respect. The respect comes for the body of information. A music teacher approaches this exalted language with care, sensitivity, and erudition. The respect comes for the process. Learning music is a lifetime endeavor. It is hard and rewarding. The respect comes for the musical products; the pieces.

These great gifts that the composers have left to us are examples of a profoundly thoughtful and generously given heritage. These creations/works allow us to enter into conversation with the great minds of Western Music. Through our example we teach ways of listening to and appreciating these meaningful musical expressions.

The teacher has respect for the teachers who once guided him with the principles of quality teaching and caring. Teachers must respect the students, themselves engaged on this quest. And there is respect for the parents. The parents are so often driving and paying, frequently when they wish it was they themselves who were taking the lessons.

There is respect for the instruments. All instruments must be treated with care.

The appropriate attitude for the piano teacher is one of caring mingled with respect. This translates into being supportive and loving. Because this is such a difficult path, each student must know the teacher is on his side, rooting for him, and thrilled with his advancement.

The appropriate attitude for the music teacher is one of "creative-impulsive." It is important to take time, get to know one's students, and make jokes! The study of music, successfully, takes place when there is time for quality exchange between the student and teacher. A "nose to the grindstone" attitude might create a pianist more quickly, but there will be no fun in it and the student will probably quit as soon as possible. The teacher must create space for the character of the student pianist to emerge. This respect for character development will manifest itself in the student's creativity, both as a composer and as an interpreter.

The appropriate attitude for the piano teacher is one of discipline coupled with support. It is important to structure the class so that all of the rigorous demands are met. Examples of these would include scales and arpeggios, Czerny, learning to read, understanding musical dynamics, and initial instruction in theoretical precepts. And these examples need to be taught in such a way as to feel free, fun and not pressured.

There is a place for pressure between teacher and student. Pressure should be applied with caution. The teacher must be able to read the student in order to know when it is appropriate. If a student is practicing and advancing there is no rush. The study of music is long term. It is to be enjoyed, and the struggle is to be enjoyed, in a rational and paced way. There is no need to put a student on a strict schedule of expectations. This is often counterproductive. When the process is enjoyed and learning becomes an end in itself, product follows with great effect and frequently exceeds all expectations.

When is it appropriate to apply pressure? The most obvious example of this is when a Student Gathering is coming up. People feel better about themselves when they are able to carry through and perform in front of others. Therefore it is important to teach the student how to perform. In this case if the student is resisting, it is good to apply pressure. Here are some examples:

"I know you want to be able to feel really good about yourself when we have the show. In this case, you had better begin practicing a lot more, so that you have your material under control."

"During the class today I am going to show you how to practice. Do this piece hands alone. Do the right hand three times. Now do the left hand 3 times. Now do this hands together 3 times. Do you see what we are doing? We are practicing. We are learning how to sit at the keyboard and study."

Unfortunately sometimes the teacher is forced to pressure the student because of the uncompromising attitude of the parents. (Read expectations here.) Musical training becomes reduced to a monetary exchange as in, "I'm not paying for this if Johnnie does not practice."

This is flawed reasoning because a person needs to learn how to practice and how to be comfortable learning. It is a maturing process.

Sometimes a teenager needs to take a break from practice. The teacher can apply pressure if the break goes on too long, but sometimes people just need to THINK about what they are doing. Thought is an intrinsic part of the musical experience. All that time alone with one's instrument is a valuable precursor to self reflective and philosophical thought. If teacher reads the student correctly, time can be taken to think. And then practice must be reinstated.

Once the process focuses mostly on parent and child, the teacher's primary role is compromised and consequently the student will probably derive little benefit from the lessons. One of the teacher's jobs is to keep parents out of the loop. Many parents want this. They appreciate the teacher taking responsibility for the student's practice and learning. These are rare and treasured parents. These parents express their trust and respect for the teacher.

Some parents cannot leave their kids alone. Sometimes the child will rebel by refusing to practice. Sometimes the parent will have financial concerns that she is not getting "her money's worth." Then the learning process has taken a curve away from the main reason the person is studying to begin with.

In conclusion, view yourself as a strict teacher. Make sure that you teach your material in a progressive and comprehensive order. The manner although, in which you teach your student, does not have to be "strict." It can be kind, respectful and serious, with room for personality, sense of humor and the serious fun of learning and creating.

Reading The Student

How do we make appropriate decisions regarding our students?

How do we decide when to progress to the next piece? How do we structure the work load? When is it appropriate to apply pressure? When do we stress practice? When do we bring parents into the process?

There are signposts that we can follow as we learn to read our students. Consider the matter of age.

When a student is young, and just starting out in private lessons, it is important to understand where he is developmentally. Many very intelligent people have trouble grasping linear concepts at a young age purely because their brains have not yet developed that skill. Most people learn the same material faster at the age of 7, than at the age of 5. And yet, for some small folks it is the right timing to begin private lessons earlier. This might be a very young child that shows tremendous interest in the piano and is talented and receptive to the teaching.

The teacher's and the parents' expectations have to be in line with the child's abilities.

Talk about practice, for instance. Be matter of fact about the need to sit at the piano at least 3 times a week for 5 minutes, or alternatively, so that, "You can do your scales, arpeggios(or finger exercises) and pieces, 3 times each."

Most little people do not exactly understand what practicing is. Occasionally I ask the parents, with the child's permission received by me beforehand, if they would be so kind as to remind the student to practice 3 times weekly.

Never push too hard at this point. Playing piano is a physical and emotional pleasure. It is tiring for the young student to concentrate. Short doses of concentration are ideal to get a person going.

Other than asking the parents to remind the child, discourage parents from interfering with practice in any way. If little Johnny just wants to sit at the piano and daydream, or make music up, that is fine. Process always takes precedence over product. This is especially important at a young age.

A marvelous attitude for teacher is:

"I am not trying to force genius. A person's talent becomes evident as he gains the skills to express it. The end result is a person able to connect with the creativity he carries within. The end result is a person educated in the musical language who can express himself with beauty and profundity. The end result is a feeling of satisfaction, gratitude, and perseverance."

When a child is pushed to immediate material gain, e.g. the piece, and how it should sound, a terrible risk is being taken. So often it is that very child who will turn around as a teenager, rebel and say, "I am never going to take another piano lesson."

Pacing the information is critical to the development and emotional comfort of the student. Some people want challenge and difficulty. Other students want to go carefully and thoroughly over their material. When the material is correctly paced, there is a happy medium between these two approaches. Whether to lean more to one side or the other depends on the character and the capacity of the student.

There are personality types. Some people are more competitive than others and relish the idea of getting a new piece each week. Others are hesitant to take on new music. These students prefer to work at pieces until they understand them very well.

It is important to listen to one's student. This is the primary way to get a "read" on your student and to adjust the schedule, or pace, of his learning. Your student will tell you what his or her style is by the way she reacts to the material.

Whatever the style, there are times when it will be appropriate to contradict it by pushing your student in the opposite direction, and there will be times to submit to it.

Sometimes it is important to slow the competitive person down. Ask him to repeat certain pieces in order to teach him discipline and patience.

For the hesitant student, apply pressure and encourage more speed. The student wants to hold on to the piece because she feels insecure. Holding on to the piece makes her feel better. She feels capable. Acknowledge this and at the same time encourage the student to let go and move on to more music.

Take a young student, beginning to learn to read music. This can occur before that person has learned to read words. To begin at the beginning, when one is so young, is to guarantee a comfort with the musical language as one grows up.

When the student arrives for her lesson have a chat. Ask her, "What's new?"

The young students generally cannot come up with anything. Persist.

"Come on," I say. "There's got to be something new."

With the older students ask about school. If possible remember the narrative from the week before and continue with, "And how did you do on that test?" etc.

With the adults ask about their kids, jobs, whatever. Sometimes begin the lesson by asking, "So how did the practicing go this week?"

The musical experience is a microcosm of one's world experience. Each person brings their personality with all of it's quirks to the study of music. Because the experience is so profound, we are our own laboratory of feelings, thoughts, structure and style.

Teacher is the chronicler of the interior event. When a student learns a piece of music, feels it deeply, and is able to perform it, teacher and student share a rare moment of insight and beauty. All of the student's work is acknowledged. The deep feelings the student has for the music are acknowledged. This unique sharing between teacher and student reaffirms the student's interior musical life and how it is brought out into the world of the senses.

Connecting with the student on a personal level increases the trust between teacher and student. It is another way of saying, "I'm listening." And this is one of the most important services a teacher can offer. Teachers listen for a living. Critical, thoughtful compassionate listening is a gift to one's student and a gift to one's self.

As a student gets older, her relationship to the piano, her music, and herself grows along with her understanding. At this time, the mechanisms for practice are already in place.

There is a qualitative difference between the pieces that are learned as part of the musical process, and the pieces that are singled out for performance. It is not necessary for each and every piece to be played with total excellence.

Most pieces can be learned, the student gleaning the more important aspects of the piece, then moving on. The pieces that are chosen for performance are the ones that are profoundly considered via all aspects of the musical experience. The more advanced the student, the longer it takes to master the complex pieces. Taking this into account, the emphasis is on the pleasure of learning a piece inside out.

The work load for the older student must correspond with other activities. Although I consider music to be the number #1 activity in my student's lives, their parents do not always agree! Therefore, school generally comes first. Then there is music and either a sport or religious school.

Stress to the parents that it is very important not to overload the kids with too many after school activities. This sometimes happens in urban areas where there is an abundant cornucopia of cultural events.

It is important to realize that the learning of music takes psychic energy as well as literal physical energy. Students spend a lot of time thinking about their pieces and thinking about the music. And the problems the music presents. And the composer that created the music. And the challenges and responsibilities to these composers.

When a person is too booked up, it is difficult to become a good musician. The practice load has to take into account the students' other activities.

A meaningful suggestion to some students is the shifting of practice time to morning instead of evening. In the morning there is nothing more glorious than sitting down at your instrument and playing. It is akin to hearing the birds sing. One's mind has not yet become cluttered with the flotsam and jetsam of daily life. One's ears have not yet been accosted by the sounds in the lunchroom cafeteria. It is a purer time of day and focusing is at a maximum. Teach early in the day for the same reasons. When a student can switch practice time to the morning, she gets a jump on the material.

For the adult student, all of the above is true. The student will let you know just how much material she can tolerate. If you push too hard, you are apt to get it right back!

Adult students also need help learning how to schedule practice time for themselves. When adults have small children, there are strategies for creating practice time. Children can be taught to sit quietly and listen. They can also be encouraged to go somewhere else.

Adult time at the keyboard is the time the adult student refreshes and replenishes himself spiritually. Children gain a great deal by the role modeling the parent portrays - serious concentration on a difficult task. This is so different than seeing Mom and Dad in front of the TV!!

Beginning With The Young Child

I teach a variety of different classes, to budding musicians of all ages. Despite the developmental and attentional considerations that must be taken into account when teaching students of differing age and musical experience, certain principles are held constant in The Music Studio. The most important of these is the mutual respect that is maintained among the students and between the students and the teacher. Our studio is a community that is based on common respect and listening. This allows the storm within to be calmed and its energy harnessed into the expressive outlet of music. The musical language created in the studio opens new venues to communication and consciousness, allowing for constant expansion in new directions.

Children taking classes in my studio are commonly divided into groups of three students of similar age. Let me describe a class session with the youngest children, ranging in age from three to five years old. The class is thirty minutes long. This class session will serve as the framework of development for the teaching. A half hour is an ideal time for the short attention spans of younger folk. Age three is a wonderful age for most children to begin because they have achieved some mastery of small motor coordination.

The children begin their lesson seated in a row at the piano keyboard. The first lesson with these children consists of acquainting the students with the keyboard. The structure of the piano keyboard, keyboard geography, allows for easy visual recognition of patterns within the keys. First, the children are told to focus their attention on the black notes. Can they see that there are groups of two black notes and groups of three black notes? The children can easily demonstrate their comprehension by finding all the groups of two and three black notes on the keyboard. They next find all the Ds on the keyboard, after being shown that D is the white note that lives in the middle of the group of two black notes. Next comes C, the white note that lives next to D and in front of the group of the two black notes. After finding all the C's on the keyboard, the children find middle C by choosing the C that is the closest to the center of the keyboard.

This much knowledge already brings a sense of achievement to these young individuals. The children can make sense of the keyboard, and can recognize notes on the keyboard and demonstrate their new knowledge to parents and friends. Note that the children are introduced from the start to the whole keyboard, and not just a selected range of the keys that are played most often. These children most likely will already have been introduced to the idea of patterns in school or preschool. Finding patterns on the keyboard thus allows them to reinforce their knowledge. At the same time it expands their understanding of this concept.

Next, a simple finger pattern is introduced to the children. The notes that the children already know are numbered, "Let's make D #2, then C will be #1. The note above D (E) will be #3."

I do not stress the note name for #3. This will come in time. The children are acquainted with their first piano tune, "Hot Cross Buns." The pattern for this tune is as follows: 3-2-1,3-2-1,1-1-1-1,2-2-2-2,3-2-1. Depending on the age and comfort level of the children I might teach the entire pattern at once, or alternatively break it up into a smaller fragment, such as 3-2-1,3-2-1. The children replicate the pattern, and soon can produce their first recognizable sound on the piano—a thrilling moment.

Every class period in the studio incorporates not only structured keyboard exercises but time for the students to produce music of their own creation. This introduces children to the first seeds of improvisation. One method that I use to introduce children to improvisation is storytelling. I take a theme and weave a story around it. The idea for the day's theme might be inspired by an approaching holiday, or a toy a student has brought to class, or even an interesting t-shirt a child is wearing! As I'm telling the story, at different points I will pause and ask a child to illustrate what is happening in the story, using the piano as the artist's canvas. At times, all the children will play at once, on different parts of the keyboard—for example, to illustrate a pounding storm. At other points in the story, one child might be the illustrator as the other children listen, expressing, for example, the sound of a kitten crying. There is NO TALKING at all from the students as the story is being told. The emphasis is on listening and playing. Imagine the scene for a moment. Very small people are seated at the piano. They are listening to the story. They are listening to themselves play the piano. They are listening to their friends playing the piano. And they are listening to the others playing when they themselves are playing as well.

Apart from storytelling improvisation, the students spend some time during each class making up music alone at the piano, as their classmates listen. One child sits at the keyboard and the others sit on the floor around the bench.

This is not only beneficial for the child improvising at the moment, who learns the freedom to express herself creatively using the whole keyboard, but it is instructive for the classmates who are not improvising at the time. These children learn what it is to listen to each other. They learn how to be good attentive audience members. The children also learn how to show each other the respect that they, in turn, desire and receive.Watching others improvise is a collective learning experience, a highly effective means of passing on ideas. If one child crosses his hands during an improvisation, I might remark on it with interest, and the other children will want to try it too.

I request only two things at the beginning from my young improvisers. One is that they listen to the sounds they are creating, and two is that they give me a good ending. I as the listener insist on being musically told when the improvisation has ended. The children are told that there are many ways to let listeners know that a piece has reached its end. Regardless of which ending they choose, they must make sure that the listener is musically aware of the piece ending.

A student begins to immediately own his sound and take responsibility for his touch. I stress endings rather than beginnings because the young improviser does not usually have an idea of what his sound will be. As he sits at the piano and develops this sound, and listens to it, the act of deciding when to end it will clarify his conscious behavior at the piano. As I explain, "Don't keep me hanging there. I want to know when you are finished."

The moment the sound begins the student can begin to construct and envision the body and the ending of a piece.

"You can end it short and sharp. You can end it slow and dreamy. You can end it by hitting a high note."

The are many options. Each child takes a turn at solo improvisation during the lesson. By the end of this segment, we are usually about 20 minutes into the class.

At the beginning of the year a child improvises for under a minute and usually does not understand what he is doing. By the end of a school year, when I say, "Wrap it up", the student produces a well-structured ending. He can go on improvising for five plus minutes lost in the beauty of the sound he is creating. At the words, wrap it up, I get my well thought out ending.

What happens to a child who learns this way? She gets to own her experience. Music is not something that is superimposed on her. Music is not that book with all the dots in it. It is the authentic creation of expressive language and it belongs immediately to each person who is fortunate enough to have an artistic experience validated.

It is now time to turn to the other instruments in the studio. The choice of which instruments are used on a particular day is often decided based on the mood of the day or of the mood of students. Suppose the students are 3 little kids, itchy with energy. I'll say, "Let's go the the drums and rock and roll!"

I allow the children to play as loudly as they like. I often join in. In society, we are frequently told to be quiet. We so often tell our children to be quiet. Here in The Music Studio, empowered by our energy, sound, instruments and teacher, the pure thrill carries us buoyantly. The old adage of "seen but not heard" is turned on its head, and there is this pure rush of energy, sound, fury and delight. After a few moments of this tide of energy we settle down to do a band activity.

For the band we choose quieter instruments. We could use marimba, claves and shekere, for instance (see pages 98-99). We take turns at first, each person experimenting on his instrument, the rest listening. Then I tell each person when to begin playing, based on who is playing the softest (most quiet) instrument. In this basic class we are listening to our own instruments at the same time as our goal of listening to one another. Then we play as an ensemble.

The class is interactive. There is a great deal of sharing. Most of our conversation is about the instruments, the sounds, and what we are doing together. Although I am a strict teacher because I have expectations that must be met, there is a current of joy and discovery that runs through class time.

Self esteem is enhanced. An interactive class promotes the ability to learn from others and get excited about what others do. Positive learning in this environment teaches a person how to be comfortable performing in front of other people. When the positive is accentuated, the class becomes more about growth and less about mistakes.

How do we teach counting? Counting is organic. Our inherent sense of timing emanates from our solar plexus, our balance and our symmetry. Rather than introduce intellectual concepts about time, encourage the children to feel the music in their bodies as they play and to move when they play their instruments.There is a natural organic connection to the music, a pulse to the rhythm/beat that is evoked when the sound is produced.

"Move when you play. Close your eyes. Listen. See if you can fit your beat inside my beat."

The only beat I am comfortable naming with the youngest students is the count of 1-2-3-4. Everybody can count to four, and everyone is comfortable with the number four. As we are working with the percussion instruments in a group, we do rhythm training by taking rhythm sticks and playing them together with an even four beat count. Once we have established the same beat, I introduce other patterns, still within the basic beat of four, that the children listen to and match with me. I might change my pattern to 1-2-3-rest, then to 1-2-rest-rest. At each stage, the children listen to my pattern and match it in sync with me. Other patterns could be 1-rest-3-rest, or 1-rest-rest-4. These patterns are learned gradually, over the course of a year of study. Each time the children grasp a more complex pattern, I tell them how smart they are or how lucky I am to be able to be teaching them. I pour love, attention and joy into the children's accomplishments at every stage of their learning process, praising them and acknowledging them for each courageous step into musical creativity.

Class is over. I say to the children, "What do I want to hear?"

They respond with, "Thank you for teaching me, Sheli."

Our studio is based on common respect, listening, joy in grappling with a difficult quest and beauty. Our structure is that great vast world of music, our language, a language of profound complexity, our finer selves always being stretched in new learning directions. In The Music Studio, the student behaves. He treats others respectfully. The student calms the storm within and harnesses its energy. With our musical instruments and musical language binding us together as one, we create a multi-cultural musical community all our own.

THE ADULT STUDENT

Entering the learning process can often create stress. Be aware that adults can regress and become anxious. If the adult has studied as a child, explore how that experience went for her. Listen to what did not work for her as a child, and use that information to assist your teaching process. Inevitably, suppressed or inherent psychological traits surface. The learning process becomes a microcosm acting as a metaphor for the student's life.

Once seated at the piano bench the student is exposed with nowhere to run and nowhere to hide. The person's inner nature—whatever it is—will most likely emerge during the course of lessons. Here the adult sits alone with herself, the instrument, and her teacher.

As the learning process begins, and she observes herself in the difficult position of being a beginner, there is a momentary feeling of panic. Self doubt sets in. But when that is overcome and learning begins in earnest, there are other more profound issues that surface.

Adults are adept, good at what they do. They are used to taking charge, calling the shots, being well organized and articulate. The study of piano for the adult beginner is an immediate challenge to all of the above. The well developed personae that guide adults through the activities in their lives are of very little use here. The adult student is confronted by his basic abilities. A simple finger exercise can be challenging and potentially upsetting.

What frames this learning experience? Generally the beginning adult student feels a paralyzing self-consciousness. A normally erudite highly educated person has an attack of self-doubt. The questions begin. "Can I really do this? Do I really want to do this? Aren't I too old to do this? Why am I doing this anyway? I don't really have time to practice," and so on.

It takes great courage, perseverance and a belief in oneself, to surmount these emotional obstacles. The student must grapple with this state of mind from the very beginning in order to successfully perform the music teacher's task.

We teachers must create a safe haven where our students feel supported and loved. We must construct an emotional habitat where our students feel safe; safe to make mistakes, safe to feel foolish, safe to once again learn as they once learned as children. When students feel ashamed or upset that they have made mistakes I say, "Every mistake is an opportunity."

"You're not Mozart. Why should you be able to do this perfectly?"

"If you didn't make mistakes you wouldn't be here with me."

"You are in the company of the greatest minds humankind has ever produced."

Many times an extra degree of compassion is called for. The inner judgmental voice of the adult beginner can persist with great tenacity. He feels demoralized and frustrated. It is at this time that teacher needs to be especially kind and caring. Reduce the expectation until the student can do whatever you are presenting (physically). Support him by telling him that he is doing well and teach him to improvise.

In this way the adult, feeling supported and free to move about the keyboard without fear of error or critique, becomes more comfortable. Over time the voice inside diminishes and the true act of listening begins.

Here is a common adult student story:

"I took lessons when I was young. I hated my teacher but loved the piano. The teacher was too strict. I never got any encouragement only criticism. But I think I might have been good."

This particular student came to lessons with great yearning and trepidation. Then as she began to study the feelings from her childhood surfaced. She loved reconnecting to the piano and yet she was bossy and rebellious with me. She informed me that she did not need to learn the left hand bass clef. She said she only wanted to learn chords. She was not keen on reading music. And, she said, she'd practice when *she* wanted.

I began by teaching her a few scales, which she remembered from childhood. Then I taught her some simple Blues patterns I IV V (see page 40). After some weeks of practicing and experimenting with improvisation, I casually took out a book of Clementi Sonatinas. I said to her, "A well rounded musical menu gives you a chance to taste many different plates. Why not just check this out, no strings attached?"

She had a gleam in her eye. Was this a trick? Who was this teacher, anyway? And better question, who now was she? She took the music and played the first few bars in the right hand. Who could not fail to be charmed by Clementi's cheerful and gracious music? And although not too difficult to play, it sounded complex and important. This was gratifying. She was hooked.

"Well, I suppose I can work on it,"she said.

We then went over the bass clef, "just a little bit" to reacquaint her with A C E G.(All Cows Eat Grass. Definitely one of my all time favorites for quick study). The next week she came back all smiles.

"I was getting a little bored with the blues anyway," she confided.

Today, five years later, she is playing advanced music on the piano and the harpsichord, composing and enjoying her process. She still has her moments. (Don't we all?)

I tell her how proud I am of how far she has come in her development as a musician and in her enjoyment of herself as a person. "All adults have busy lives. You are doing your best."

Thus reassured, she continues her studies with grace and good will. (By the way, she is older than I am by a good many years.)

Here is the story of a very successful man. He was educated, extremely articulate and awfully busy. His love of music and literature had led him to piano lessons. On a deeper level his yearning for beauty had led him to the world of music. Oft times men are so busy taking care of business that the spiritual side of their lives goes wanting. This man yearned for a way to step into the cycle of beauty, which is the creative quest.

Hard and accomplished in so many ways, when he played Chopin he was able to relax into a softer space. By giving him the tools to reach this moment of spiritual refreshment, I, as his teacher, got to participate in a profound intimate moment with him. Connecting with The Muse, learning the musical language, is difficult. The rewards are numerous- beauty, delight, rejuvenation. His daily struggle became a focus point for him of groundedness and fulfillment.

Many men want this. Most do not articulate this urge to connect with one's own creativity in a way not connected with money, power or worldly attention. This need can be satisfied by the study of music.

Our lives are taken up by many details and mundane concerns. We need to deal with these details, but when we are practicing, we have a respite from triviality. We are giving ourselves the chance to refine our thought process by the very complexity of the task we undertake.

One day a woman came to me, recommended via friends, to study piano. She was a very goal directed incisive person. Her credits included a PhD and a black belt in Karate. Her small motor coordination was precise and effective. Her restlessly inquisitive intelligent mind eagerly learned and absorbed all I taught her. And yet the idea of performing in the twice yearly adult Student Gatherings filled her with fear even though she was more than capable of the performance. Her problem was a fear of exposing herself in the process. She felt vulnerable.

We began dealing with this by talking about it. She was very brave and willing to take a look at how she felt. Revelations about her childhood helped her to understand her fears.

Slowly, I began to move my chair further away from the keyboard. She got progressively more nervous the farther away from the piano I got. I became more like an "audience" and less like her trusted teacher as I moved farther into the room.

Although she had a high powered job, requiring her to make presentations, she was never comfortable doing them. Because these same feelings began to assail her at the lessons, we dealt with this in a very physical way. She began to feel more comfortable as I finally was able to sit at quite a distance from the piano.

Throughout this process I gave her much verbal encouragement. Rather than caving in to her fears, we both traveled through them together. Not only has she learned to perform with more comfort, she has lightened up. Her playing, once so controlled and elegant, is now more accessible. Still elegant, it is now more generous both in her experience of the music flowing through her and our experience of listening to her play it.

In summary, each of these examples illustrates methods for assisting the student to feel more comfortable. The fundamental ideas are those of safety, confidentiality, improvisation, kindness, and the lofty ideals that are in keeping with learning music.

An adult repertoire should have a few finished pieces in it at all times so that the student can play for family and friends at a moment's notice. This brings a feeling of competency and accomplishment to the student.

PIANO PERFORMANCE

INTRODUCTION TO TECHNIQUE

The new student comes to the studio. If it is an adult, she needs to be reassured.

"This is a very safe place. A lot of mistakes are made here." Generally this gets a laugh and an appreciative look.

Have your student sit at the keyboard and get acquainted with her. Look your student in the eye. It is important to connect personally and let her know that you are there because you care.

Take the student's hand in yours and gently pinch the fatty part of each of her fingers. "This is the part of the finger you play the note with. It is where you will have the most control over your notes. Too high up on your finger and you slip, like being on tiptoes. The hand comes into the keyboard at an angle, like a plane landing."

The wrists are slightly elevated so that the fingers have maximum movement. The hand is then placed on the keyboard, with the fifth finger on C (left hand). The student is encouraged to rock his hand back and forth, feeling the movement emanating from the wrist rotation. Then the student places his thumb on C in the right hand. The hand rotates at the wrist so that the student becomes acquainted with the feeling of the wrist rotation as well.

The wrist plays an integral part in piano technique. Wrist flexibility allows the fingers increased articulation and tonal and technical variety. Here is an excellent technique for training.

The first technique is the *llave* movement. This means *key* in Spanish. Ask the student to pretend that he is turning a key in a lock. Watch the way the wrist rotates. To teach this, talk to the student about going from macro to micro. When something is played slowly, using this technique, like a figure in Czerny, the movement is quite large. As the speed increases the size of the movement diminishes so that the wrist, at speed, is now moving quickly and deftly. The unwieldy movement produced when the figure is played slowly, gives way to a lighter quicker action. This wrist movement is helpful for speed, trills, ornaments, and many of the technical features repertoire presents.

Another beneficial technique is called the *cajon* movement. In this context, *cajon* in Spanish means *drawer*. The movement is likened to that of opening and closing a drawer. The arm moves back and forth at the keyboard. When this technique is practiced until it can be done quickly, a scratching effect is produced on the keys. The fingers pull back quickly as the arm retracts. This valuable technique is another aid for speed, octaves etc.

Many students move when they are playing piano. As long as the foot is not tapping, this is fine. The pulse must be felt. Frequently it comes through the solar plexus and a student will make circular movements with her torso as she plays. The movement should not interfere with the quality of the sound, or become distracting for the listener.

Students forget to breathe. We all hold our breath when we are trying to accomplish something. It is important to remind the student to breathe. Reminding the student to breathe begins when the student begins lessons. Bringing the consciousness of breath into the experience of teaching and studying enriches the physical experience.

Beginning students tend to keep one hand on the bench while the other hand plays the keyboard. Remind the student to keep both hands close to the keyboard. Teach a student to sit in a balanced fashion so that he does not have to lean on his hands.

Ask the student to find his "sitz bones". These bones are the ones that can be felt if you sit and and rock back and forth. These are the bones that we balance on (sacrum).

Once he can identify those bones, ask him to slump forward on the bench. Now tell him that you are going to pull a thread up through the top of his head and as you pull he needs to sit up taller and taller until he is in a hyper extended military pose. You then pretend to pull this thread up. When he is as erect as possible, tell him you are going to let go and that you want him to fall back onto the bones just identified, his sitz bones, without slumping forward.

This is the correct posture for playing the piano. Using this posture, the back remains straight, the internal organs are in order, and the body is relaxed and centered.

When teaching harpsichord, explain to the student that the fingers come first, the wrist is at the command of the fingers, and the arm is at the command of the wrist. It is a very different technique than at the piano. The hands are quiet and the feel of the "pluck" determines the amount of force the finger uses. The wrists remain steady as do the arms. They are all on one level. A child can have a small stool placed under his feet so that they are not dangling in the air. This keeps the body properly balanced. The center of the keyboard and the center of the body should correspond. Because the technical demands of the harpsichord are equal to those of the piano, the student must learn posture and the student must learn a quality of "stillness" that will facilitate the difficult technique needed to produce articulation on the harpsichord. (Recommended reading Couperin, Art of the Clavecin.)

Reading Music

The book of music is taken out. For the very young student, she traces her hands at the beginning of the book (see recommended editions page 109) and numbers her fingers. She has already had small motor exercises and little pieces so she will be familiar with her thumb numbering 1, etc.

The student looks at a diagram of the staff. This first look at the music serves as an introduction to the visual side of the musical experience.

Take the child's right hand and hold it in the air for a moment and say, "Tada! All the notes that live in the treble clef from middle C and up are played with the right hand."

Move her hand from the middle C with a flourish on up the keyboard.The process is then repeated for the left hand.

Music is written on lines and spaces. These lines and spaces correspond to the notes, like musical steps, on the piano. Start with middle C because it is shared by both hands.

"And look, it has a line running through it." Utilize visual aids to help the student remember the note.

"Do you know where the C is in the middle of the piano? Why is it there?"

"Because the name of the piano is right above it."

"Good. That is an easy way to remember. And how about patterns? What are some of the patterns we see at the keyboard?"

"Right. We have groups of two black notes and groups of three black notes. And where does C live? Good. It lives in front of the group of two black notes. Is that true of all the C's?"

Constant reinforcement of visual patterns creates a piano keyboard geography along with the notational geography.

Beginning with the treble clef, the first three notes are taught. Show the child at the piano, and on the music, where C D and E live.

"Oh look. The C is the only note that has a line through it. The D lives "plop" under all the lines of the treble clef." (Try it. It may sound corny but the kids love that word!)

"And the E, oh wow. It lives on the first line of the treble clef." Talk about the treble clef. "The treble clef are the lines and spaces of the staff on top. The right hand plays those notes that are written in the treble clef."

Look at the music. Teach the information in this order:

"Do you see those little boxes? They are called measures. And look at the end of the piece. That is called a double bar line. And the lines that divide the boxes up are called bar-lines. How many measures or little boxes are there in this piece? What are the names of the lines that divide the little boxes? Where is the end of the piece? How do you know? Is this piece in the treble clef or the bass clef? Which hand plays this piece? What are the notes in the piece? Show me all the Cs. Show me a D. Show me an E. What happens if the note is not colored in? Hold it a little longer. Why are there little numbers on top of the notes? What do you think they are?"

If the student asks why the little boxes are called measures, explain to him that they measure time. There is no further instruction at this point about time signatures.

This is the basic material covered in the first class when the student begins to read. The same material is gone over class by class until the student learns it all.

For the adult student, the same material is covered, presented in a more mature way. The beginning adult texts are far more complex and require more intellectual ability.

Bartok wrote the Microcosmos series (see page 109) specifically to teach the adult student. This series is an alternative to institutionalized method teaching. Because Bartok used many of the melodies he gathered from his research in Hungarian folk music, the pieces have a haunting quality.

The adult student relates far better to this mature musical vision. The companion text is by Hershal Pyle, and is called The University Piano Series (see page 109). This book uses a format similar to Microcosmos. It analytically explains aspects of the musical experience in a cogent way.

As the student advances the scope of the material grows to meet the demands of the music.

How to speak about music, communicate it, and discuss it are powerful tools for the student to learn. By being able to recognize a very basic structure, the student can go home and practice the piece with the knowledge he has acquired. By looking at a piece before it is played, and by analyzing the notes and structure, the piece is easier to decipher. The student learns to discuss and analyze aspects of musical form and structure. This ability can be a powerful tool, not just for learning material which the teacher assigns, but also for the student's life long appreciation of music and other arts.

The texts recommended here are proven routes to learning. The children's beginning texts, by Thompson and Schaum, (see page 109) are comforting. Most parents see what their children begin on and they say, "Hey, I learned on that too!" That is an affirmation for child and parent alike. As soon as the child has outgrown the essential method books and can attempt to play actual compositions, start with the Anna Magdalena Notebook compiled by Anna Magdalena Bach. This notebook contains pieces that Mrs. Bach collected through-out the years from her husband, herself and their friends. When fellow musicians visited she would ask them to write something out to assist in the teaching of her many children. It is important to take a moment to discuss the relevance of the urtext edition.

Choosing editions that have come to us as directly as possible from the composer's hand are essential in the correct study of music (further discussion of the importance of urtext- page 71). Along with the Anna Magdalena Bach Notebook teach Mozart Klavierstucke (see page 110). Never teach "watered down" classics. This bastardization of the musical idea shortchanges the student. An abundance of simple, well composed music exists which the teacher can use to teach the student how to begin thinking about what she is doing. "Watered down" texts often convey misinformation about the music, such as incorrect dynamics and odd fingering.

Musical Dynamics

Music happens at the moment when a person takes what she is feeling, pours it into the keyboard, and is profoundly affected by the sound. This miraculous moment affecting student and teacher alike, is the primal experience of music making. How does the student get a musical sound? The student gets a musical sound by learning to listen.

In many cases beginning students play very softly out of fear of hitting the wrong notes. That same fear can also drive students to bang on the keys. When students learn to listen, they realize that other possibilities exist. Students realize that they can alter the sound to make it more pleasing.

The composer gives us the notes to play and includes the symbols that tell us how to play those notes. When the student is a beginner and there are no dynamic notations in her material, ask her to play the first line of the piece with more force, and the second line of the piece quietly.

"Which way did you like it better? How do you think it sounded when you played it quietly? Play the whole piece quietly now and see if you can communicate a feeling of sadness."

Experiment with different possibilities.

"Relax your wrists and hands and see if you can play it faster. Play the second phrase as though it is an echo of the phrase before it. Articulate* at the measure. Sculpt your musical sound, just as you would tell an interesting story."

Teach basic dynamics to begin with. Dynamic musical language is written in Italian. Talk about the most common dynamic symbols. F - forte; loud, MF - mezzo forte; medium loud, FF - fortissimo; very loud, P - piano; soft, MP - mezzo piano; medium soft, and PP - pianissimo; very soft. Include RIT - ritard; slow down, MODERATO; at a moderate or even pace, and WALTZ; in 3/4 time, dance like.

Sometimes it is not necessary to be too specific when discussing dynamics. Often an image - like a green rolling field, or a texture - like water bubbling in a brook, or a mood - like the tension one feels before a test, gives the student musical ideas about sculpting the sound.

With advanced students a tremendous amount of scholarship goes into the careful reading of the dynamic map of the piece. Each phrase, bar line, figure, accent, etc. is carefully analyzed. The scholarship that goes into the minute tracking of the dynamic map is thoughtful and informed by the era.

Begin by looking up when the composer lived and died. If possible, identify when the piece was written. If a piece by Mozart is being played, and it was composed after 1770, this is a piece written for fortepiano. Discuss the characteristics of the keyboard for this time period. Note that the construction of the instrument was much lighter. The fortepiano resembled it's predecessor the harpsichord because the same materials were being used to build both instruments. The exception was that the fortepiano strings were hammered rather than plucked.

What effect did this have on dynamics and why is it relevant today? Within the context of Mozart's sound, it is appropriate to "tone down" the dynamic range the modern piano is capable of. Because the earlier instrument was made of lighter materials, the touch and the intensity of volume were both affected. Full speed was possible.

When we consider speed, in the 18th century people were not experiencing speed the way we do today. There were no telephones, cars, computers or airplanes. The pace of life was slower, more gracious, geared perhaps to the heartbeat and the body's ability to run. Horses and carriages were the quickest transport method.

Therefore an argument can be made that the speed with which we play on contemporary keyboards should not be so fast that the integrity of the phrase becomes an egotistical blur. Instead, our style and technique should acknowledge the gracious tempo and dynamics which past composers derived from the instruments of their times.

The fortepiano offers many choices for musical dynamics. One can express articulation, as well as the style of the classical period that transitioned into the romantic period. As we transpose this information onto the modern day piano, the playing is altered slightly to bring the composer's original intention into focus.

There are dynamic renderings that are appropriate to each musical period. It is essential to understand music in it's historical context to teach these dynamics. Once they are understood, and experimented with on the modern piano, it is possible to play them while remaining faithful to the composer's vision of the piece.

In the early part of our century it was all the rage for editions to "improve" on the works of the Great Masters. In the editors' defense, this was often done in the hope that further editing would make it easier for the student to perform the music on the modern keyboard.

There was also a trend to "romanticize" or reinterpret earlier music to fit a later musical idea or construct. As a result many bastardized musical editions appeared in the marketplace. In my opinion this has had a deleterious effect on many of the teachers who were trained between the years of 1900-1970.

Take a look at the phrasing that occurs in a piece by Mozart. When looked at carefully, in an urtext edition, there is very little phrasing. The rules of the baroque period, the period preceding Mozart, were still in place, although beginning to fade.

Mozart included few dynamic markings in his works. The predominant aesthetics of the time emphasized clarity of structure, with clearly delineated sections and forms. These, for the most part, defined the use of dynamics. Within that context, Mozart began developing the melodic fragments which we now recognize as the first types of pianistic phrases.

He slurred over the bar line infrequently. There aren't many F and P signs. Sometimes there is phrasing within the bar. When it is played as written, it evokes baroque articulation. His music became a new exploration of this keyboard, the fortepiano, where dynamics could be emphasized because the keys were being hammered rather than plucked, and because he could now use a pedal. Sustaining the sound for longer periods than the rapid decay on the harpsichord offered new compositional possibilities for overtones and drama.

The new features on the fortepiano were fun. Mozart was born in 1756, right as this major shift was to take place between instruments. He was a child of the baroque, and a profound and innovative adult classicist.

His knowledge about instruments began just as he began composing. Mozart traveled over much of Germany staying at the homes and palaces of the very rich. He saw all the latest musical inventions and played them. His ever inquiring genius recorded all of the advances in keyboard development.

But his instrument at home was his trusty harpsichord. After all, the harpsichord had been queen for 200 years. (1575 - 1775)

Our dynamics are informed by our musical knowledge. It is not enough to have a 19th-20th Century understanding of how to play piano. It is not enough, in other words, to know what forte means. Forte must be understood in the context of, "Which composer? When did he live? Where did he live? Which instrument was he playing on? Who were his peers? What part did the music play in the lives of the people? What were they dancing? How did they worship? Who was the King?"

Why is this relevant for the modern day piano? The modern piano has many dynamic capacities. One can do anything on it. The range is tremendous. Pedals provide a lush quality to the sound. Why not just take the old Masters and play them any way one wants to? Why spend so much time learning the circumstances of each composer?

The answer is aesthetic. There is a need to preserve the original voices of our greatest minds. We can take Mozart onto the modern piano. We will also take the precepts that come to us from his era so that we can play his divinely inspired music the way he intended.

The serious teacher will grapple with these fascinating questions. A good beginning would be to begin to learn about the age the composer lived, what kind of instrument he composed for, and how that instrument was played. Researching these three fundamental concerns of teachers everywhere will increase the joy, depth and intellectual development of learning dynamics.

TIME SIGNATURES

Human beings seem to be most comfortable with the number four. Perhaps it is because we have 2 hands and 2 legs, or 2 eyes and 2 ears. We frequently divide our monetary system into the number 4, four quarters to a dollar. There is a comfort in the rhythmic pattern of 4. The youngest child to the oldest adult can relate to it.

When the time signature is taught from the inside out, counting is an organic experience. For instance, tell your students when they are first learning how to read, to hold the "not colored in notes" a little longer. With only that much information, a student rarely takes a timing misstep. It is easy to feel the count of 4, easy to intuit it. Rather than intellectualize the experience by taking it outside of the body and bringing it to aural consciousness through the eyes and brain, let the students begin by feeling it and hearing it. The innate sense of rhythm that is the heritage of each human being is often misdirected by anxiety about not understanding how to count.

Often adults who were once music students, will complain about their previous experience by saying, "I could never count. I never understood time signatures. Counting drove me crazy."

This is an important tenet of The Sheli Nan Method. Students learn later on how to intellectually explain time signatures. They begin by feeling the music internally and hearing it externally. When a student has a piece in 3 and plays it in four, by holding the last note of each measure too long, play it for her so that she can hear and feel the rhythm of three. "Three just keeps going. It is like a dance. Do not stop at the end of the measure. Feel it like this."

Depending on the age and development of the student, do not introduce time signatures for a year or two. It is important to pace the material so that it can be absorbed according to each person's learning ability. There is no rush. Studying and playing music is a cumulative experience. The more a student practices the more she learns.

The same is true for listening and thinking. This ongoing process of the accumulation of knowledge allows for the comforting thought that all students will arrive at one point or another, not necessarily at the same time, or together. People have their own learning pace. This is healthy and just.

When the time comes, draw a circle. Draw two intersecting lines. Tell your student that you have just drawn a pie and then color in one of the pieces. "This pie is just like a whole note. It is worth four beats, like four pieces of pie, (or four quarters in the dollar)."

Hold a note down on the piano and count four beats. Then play four quarter notes. Explain to the student that the duration of the sound is what determines the whole note sound from the quarter note sound. Go on to explain the half note and the dotted half note.

After playing piano and percussion for a year or two, this information is easy to synthesize and understand. Continue the teaching.

"So you see, all the time we were talking about the little boxes or measures, we were talking about measuring time. At the beginning of the piece you have two numbers. These numbers are called your time signature. Let's only look at the top number today. The top number is 3. This means that there are three beats in the measure. Let's take a look at that and see if we can identify all of the beats."

This is happening for the child who has graduated out of the baby beginner books and is now playing pieces in two hands. His age is about seven or eight. (It can take longer depending on the learning curve of the individual student.)

It is gratifying to see these concepts absorbed by the student. Stress is no longer a factor. The learning becomes a confirmation of the child's intuition. From there it is a gentle progression into more complex timing. Everything makes sense.

When teachers push the intellectual information about time signatures at the very beginning of the learning experience some people flounder, obsess and miss the interior signals that give them access to their natural sense of rhythm.

As the student progresses teach her the time signature formula. With this formula the student can never go wrong. Occasionally, with younger children, it is appropriate to only explain the top number. The entire formula can be illustrated for the younger student as she matures at the keyboard.

THE TIME SIGNATURE IS 2/4 WHICH MEANS THAT THERE ARE TWO BEATS PER MEASURE AND THE QUARTER NOTE GETS ONE COUNT.

Ask the student to memorize this. Explain to her that it is not a fraction but two numbers that each have different meanings. The top number refers to the beats in the measure and the bottom number gives her the valuation of the notes that are to be counted. Have her substitute 3/4 within the time signature formula, then 6/8, and 3/2. Have her explain exactly what that means. Now the student is well educated and clear about the instructions that the time signature gives.

SCALES

One of the first concepts that is taught to the student of any age is that of the octave, 8 notes. The piano is described as made up of patterns. The main pattern is the octave. Have the student identify the octave from middle C to high C. Count the notes. Find other octaves in C. Then find a D, (the white note between the group of two black notes - another prominent pattern). Count the notes between Ds. This is piano geography.

When the student is comfortable with this simple concept, introduce the scale. "A scale is a way to get through an octave. How many fingers do I have? How many notes are there in the scale? What are some of the ways I can divide up my fingers to equal eight? 5+3? Excellent."

Always ask your students as many questions as you can. Even simply answered questions provide a feeling of empowerment.

"So this is the way we do it. In the right hand, we play 1-2-3 then we put our thumb under and continue with 1-2-3-4-5. Now let's play the scale back. Let's try the left hand now. 5-4-3-2-1 and now put your third finger over your thumb to complete with 3-2-1.Pretend you are the Dad and your fingers are the kids. The kids have to obey!"

If the student is able to, he now plays the scale hands alone and hands together. He is asked to practice each hand 3 times daily. Depending on his age and ability he can also practice the scale 3 times hands together. He can play anywhere on the keyboard as long as he has only one octave in distance between his hands when he plays hands together.

In the following weeks the rest of the white note scales are taught concurrently with a SHARP CHART. This is for the youngest through the oldest student.

The next scale taught is G. Say to your student, "I'm going to give you a hint. You are going to figure out the G scale. It begins on G. It has the same fingering as C, but you will hear one note that sounds off and you will need to correct it by going up onto a black note."

In this way you check the student's ear, her ability to recognize tones. The student also feels great when she figures out the new scale. Every time a new scale is about to be learned, ask the student if she can figure it out. Give her a few hints and let her try.

Then you begin to write up the sharp chart, teaching the scales in this order, adding to the sharp chart when each new scale is learned.

C	
G	f#
D	f# c#
A	f# c# g#
E	f# c# g# d#
B	f# c# g# d# a#

After B is taught and the irregular fingering in the left hand has been explained and understood, teach F. Always ask your student to play the scale and repeat the fingering both forward and back as you write it out in her book (see page 85).

When the scales have been learned in the order above, as a recognition of the student's hard work, place the scales in the order of how they show up on the piano. (C-D-E etc.)

It is now time to learn the black note scales. Teach them in chromatic order. After learning C# add this to your sharp chart leaving a space for F#. Have the student name you each note in the scale. When he says "F", then "F#", say, "Wait a minute. You can only have one F per scale. Let's stay with F# since we are in a sharp scale, C#. Can you think of another name for F natural?"

Repeat the process for B#. In this way the student realizes how all of the notes of C are sharped.

"How cool!" Make a fuss. This is definitely a one of a kind scale!

The student practices all of the white note scales, then the black note scales. If he has been doing the white note scales H.A. and H.T. (hands alone and hands together) now he can do the white note scales H.T. and the black note scales H.A. and H.T. Once the black note scales can be done H.T. as well it is time to integrate the scales. The next concrete step on the road to progress is taken. The scales are now played chromatically.

"Congratulations. You are making progress."

Soon the scales are all extended to two octaves. Learning music is the ever expanding accumulation of knowledge. The signposts that allow us to technically chart our progress bring the student joy and a sense of accomplishment.

As time goes on, the harmonic minor scales (see page 103) are taught. When this formula is discussed then it is time to talk about the major scale in its theoretical order (whole step whole step half step, whole step whole step whole step half step). First the white notes scales are taught in keyboard order, then the black note scales are taught. Then the two are integrated.

And only then does the challenging and fun next phase begin! The harmonic minor scales are then integrated into the major scales. The student plays the C major scale then the C harmonic minor scale without repeating the root note. The pattern is repeated on each note.

At this time the scales are extended to three octaves.

When this has been accomplished the student begins to learn the melodic minor scales (see page 104). These scales go up in one pattern and return in another. The student should then learn to play the scales in chromatic order, starting on successive half-steps. Once these scales are learned on their own they are then integrated into the entire scale pattern. C major, harmonic minor, melodic minor, C# major, harmonic minor, melodic minor etc. in 4 octaves. The student has arrived. Scale mastery has been achieved.

Most scales begin on the same finger. Some scales do not. For example, Eb begins on the major in 3 in the left hand and 2 in the right hand, on the harmonic minor in 2 in the left hand and 2 in the right hand and on the melodic minor in 2 in the left hand and 2 in the right hand. When this occurs teach your students to gracefully come off the note before the root note and then come down onto the correct fingers. It's like a slight hovering above the keys for only a moment as the student becomes used to the finger change.

There are many different opinions on appropriate scale speed. There is a quick technique called wrist leading where the hand is tilted forward on the way up with the wrist leading it. There is a quick turn over at the thumb juncture and the fingers graze the notes in a subtly jumpy manner. When perfected, the effect is less of a note by note playing and more of a speed blur with a slightly uneven gait. With time and practice this evens out.

Scales can become a relaxing meditation. This technique must be preceded by years of hard work of playing the scales evenly in a slower fashion. For students that passionately pursue speed, this is an effective technique. It isn't necessary to spend time and energy on the scales beyond the four octave basics.

Some teachers elaborate on basic scale patterns. They have students do scales in 3rds and 10ths for instance. This is a better exercise for advanced Conservatory students because scales exist to strengthen and warm up hands and mind.They are a means toward an end, rather than an end in themselves.

Scales and arpeggios are perhaps the most 3 dimensional structures we own in our musical language. Sure, you can't hold one in your hand, and yet the structure, solidity and identity of a scale resonates for those of us musically literate, in a way few other musical structures do. There is an architecture to the scale that provides comfort and a grounded framework. This basic musical building block is always there. Musical pieces come and go in the student's life. Improvisations and compositions come and go in the musician's life. The scale is always there.

Arpeggios

At the beginning, students seem to fall into categories.

"Oh, I've got an arpeggio girl!" It can be long fingers, particular aptitude, or the student simply preferring the arpeggios to the scales or vice versa. This evens out after awhile.

Arpeggios are another way to get through an octave. Major arpeggios are taught in 1 octave in this order. C-F-G-D-E-A-B. They are then placed in keyboard order. The left hand is always taught with the fingering 5-4-2-1 with the exception of B when it is taught as 5-3-2-1. As the fourth finger is the most difficult finger to control, it is used as often as possible. Be prepared. It is irritating to students.Take your student's left hand and put a little pencil mark on the 3rd finger. Tell him not to use that finger.

The arpeggios are taught in one octave H.A. and H.T. (hands alone and hands together) in groups of three. The arpeggio is played 3 times not repeating the top note. The wrist moves lightly through the air maneuvering the fingers into place. It is slightly elevated from the keyboard and leads forward and back. The fingers follow.

Once the student can play his arpeggios in one octave, 3 times H.T., begin on the black notes. Teach C# Eb Ab and Bb.When this fingering is taught call it "magic fingering".

"Imagine, if you use this unique fingering, your fingers will land right on the note they need to play. It's amazing." You will have students walking out of your studio saying: "Yes! I got a new arpeggio!! Yes! I got a new scale!"

F# is taught last and then the arpeggios are practiced chromatically. Students feel a sense of accomplishment as they learn their technique. They can see their progress clearly when the technique is taught in this order.

Now extend the arpeggios to 2 octaves. Then teach the minor arpeggios (see page 106). When these have been taught, and these can now be taught chromatically if the student is ready, integrate the major and minor arpeggios and extend them to three octaves.

The dominant 7th arpeggios (see page 107) are taught next. These are so much fun. Every finger is used. The sound is bluesy. The dominant 7th arpeggios are cheerful. Show the students, always, how to create chords from all of their arpeggios. This will enhance their improvisations and compositions by giving them more material and ideas.

Now it is time for the diminished arpeggios (see page 107). These are the "horror movie" arpeggios. Demonstrate them at the keyboard with the pedal down. Students like the exotic quality of these arpeggios.The student should now be capable of practicing his scales and arpeggios in four octaves. His chromatic mastery of the arpeggios goes like this. C major, minor, dominant 7th, diminished, C# major, minor, dominant 7th diminished, etc. The student has arrived!!

Once again, for the arpeggios that do not always begin on the same finger, use the technique of hovering momentarily over the root note and then coming down on the appropriate finger. The student can now do all her scales and arpeggios in a cohesive organized manner. It should take less than 10 minutes. This can be done before each practice session, or it can be broken up into scales one day and arpeggios the next. It depends on the student, his work load, and his commitment.

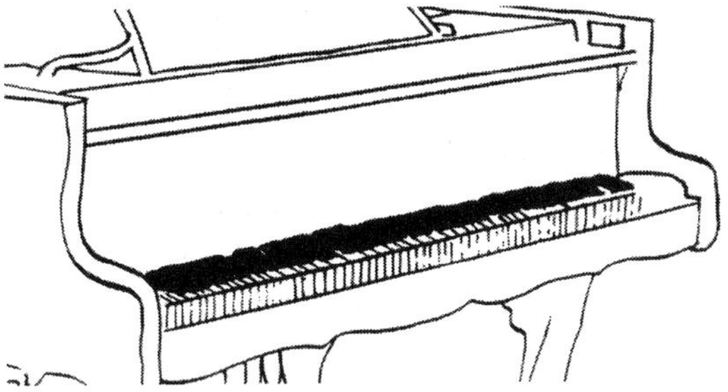

KEY SIGNATURES

Key signatures are taught in tandem with the sharp chart.

"Why do I have to learn the sharps in this order rather than the way they show up in the scale?" The answer to this is that the key accidentals which designate the key signature always appear in the same sequence in both staves following the clef sign. This is the order of the sharps that we learn in the sharp chart. If we memorize the chart like this, we will be able to identify the key signatures that much quicker. For instance:

"How many sharps are at the beginning of the piece? Two? What is the first sharp you ever learned? What is the name of the scale that has 2 sharps? What is the first note in the piece in the left hand? What is the first note of the piece in the right hand? What notes does the piece end on? Do the beginning notes in the first measure of the piece in both hands when played together, create a recognizable chord?"

Key signatures help the student recognize hand positions and piano geography.

"We are playing around in the scale of D. We are using the notes in the D scale and that includes the sharps we find in the D scale."

For the advanced student the complexity of the questions you ask might go something like this, "What key does the piece seem to be in? Does it begin with a major sound or a minor sound? If it's minor, how do we find the relative minor? What is the relative minor and what is its relationship to the major key? Can you count down three half steps? What is the first note of the piece in the left hand? What note does the piece end on?"

The relative minor key is related to the major key because the key signature is shared. By going down three half steps from the identified major key the relative minor is found. For instance, if there are two sharps at the beginning of the piece the student will identify the key of D. If she begins to play and the sound is a minor sound, and the piece, rather than beginning in D has begun in B, the piece will be in the relative minor key to D, B minor.

For the keys with flats, go over the order that the flats appear in when the scales are learned. Write this out:

F	bflat
Bb	bflat eb
Eb	bflat eb ab
Ab	bflat eb ab db
Gb	bflat eb ab db gb cb
Db	bflat eb ab db gb db fb

PERCUSSION

Western keyboard music is only about 500 years old. Music making in Africa, however, may go back 20,000 years or more. Although the industrialized world has long considered Western Classical Music the music of culture and education, African music also embodies its own unique history, development and levels of complexity.

Given Africa's immensity, one realizes how many different types of peoples, religions and cultures exist through-out the continent. However, within this diversity, there are also many commonalities in the approaches to music, especially among the various peoples of Sub-Saharan Africa.

African music has an intricacy and difficulty that make it challenging and satisfying to play. The approach to learning the music is quite different than the Western linear model. Unlike Western music, there is no one way to play an African piece because each tribe and region has had it's own customs and language. Music was indivisible from life. Music was something sacred, something secret. People created it. It was not for sale. It was not a commodity.

What once took place in the village is now increasingly an urban phenomenon. In towns people have begun to share their private dialects. The sound that has come from the village and gone into the town has now changed. It is the same note taken from the village, but there is a chemistry that has transformed the sound.

Traditional music has been affected by modern music. We are not privy to the secrets that the musicians tell when they speak through their instruments. We Westerners have been invited to participate in the great cultural wealth that is African music by those teachers generous and kind enough to share their traditions with us. Learning to speak the rhythms on percussion instruments adds greatly to the study of music and adds greatly to the study of classical music, in particular.

The first aspect of this experience is physical. Students are taught to move when they play their percussion instruments. There is a natural physical rhythm to our musical experience. Learning to "hook in" and explore the connection between rhythm and movement helps us to understand the origin of sound. As a result of this understanding, we can then appreciate music intuitively as well as intellectually.

We grow comfortable with our bodies as we strive for the beat. If we can identify the basic beat and it's four components, we begin to have a way to contextualize, conceptualize and communicate music. It is an organic experience that translates both intellectually and spiritually.

An African piece of music is a complex weave who's closest cousin is the symphony orchestra. Just as in the orchestra, the whole is the sum of the parts, the same is true of a performance of African music. It is a communal experience of the culture in which each participant plays a very specific role.

The beat is broken down into small subdivisions. Each musician is responsible for playing at a precise moment in order for the various patterns to lock in, and for the overall piece to resonate as it is meant to. It becomes a multi-dimensional listening experience, analogous to listening to the symphony.

Learning to speak the beat with percussion instruments is another way of having a conversation. Sometimes the conversation is set, and other times, like an improvisation, the conversation is created by the participants. It requires serious listening because it is only when you can hear others that you can hear yourself, and vice versa.

Very young children can learn this much needed skill. It is surprising how small children can improvise with some clarity. Specific rhythms are taught and the concept of participating in a jam* session can also be taught and understood by people of all ages.

What fun it is to communicate in this way. The students get to move their bodies. Sometimes they break into spontaneous dance. This type of rhythmic training is unparalleled. They learn to listen. And, unlike the study of piano, where one is alone with one's process and one's thoughts, this group activity balances that experience by giving students the immediate experience of communicating in their new language, the musical language.

After thoroughly explaining the 4 beats, (see page 17) the patterns become more complex. This is the next pattern taught. The right hand holds a steady beat of quarter notes counted as though in a 2/4 time signature. The count is 1 and 2 and etc. After this beat is established in the right hand and is consistent, the left hand comes in on the "and" of 2. It looks like this:

```
R.H.    1 1  1 1  1 1  1 1
        x    x    x    x

L.H.    1 1  1 1  1 1  1 1
               x         x
```

Once the person can add this second half of the second quarter-note beat to the steady right hand pattern, the next beat is taught.These beats are taught verbally and by listening and by voicing the count. It is a good idea to tap these beats out on your legs. There is no talk of time signatures at this point.

R.H. 11 11 11 11 11 11 11 11
x x x x

L.H. 11 11 11 11 11 11 11 11
x x

These two patterns can be played comfortably by two people because they lock into one another. A variety of percussion instruments can be used. The students learn both patterns and then learn to switch back and forth with one another. This can be structured in group or just with two people.

If the patterns are taught on Boomwhacker®** Percussion Tubes (see page 100), the hitting hand (right hand) can vary the sound by striking the downbeat on the lower end of the instrument (the right hand part in each pattern) with the following beat (left hand part) striking higher up on the tube.

Once mastery has been achieved with these two simple patterns the bell pattern can be added.

Let's take a look at the bell pattern and then break it down. One hand strikes and the other hand holds the instrument. It could be played on the Boomwhackers, cow bell, agogo bell, claves etc.

11 11 11 11 1 1 1 11
x xx x xx x x x xx

The way to hold claves is to cradle one stick in your left hand curling your fingers around the stick so that your fingertips grip the stick. There needs to be a pocket of space between the stick and your palm so that the produced sound can resonate. Fingers should not wrap all the way around the stick because they might get hit by the other hand when striking.

The pattern above begins with the right hand striking the "outer" higher end of the stick. The next two beats are struck further in. Then the beats alternate higher - lower on the instrument.

Tell your students to use their bodies when playing these instruments. You don't want a person all tightened up, eyes half squeezed shut, concentrating with all his might. It would be better if he were swaying his hips, relaxing his arms, and moving his shoulders.

**Boomwhackers® is a registered trademark under license to Whacky Music, Inc.

Remember, any beat can be broken up into its smallest component. The entire bell pattern does not need to be learned at once nor is it always necessary for it to be played in its entirety. It is possible for two people to share that beat. For instance, person #1 could strike:

```
1 1  1 1  1 1  1 1  1
x    xx   x    xx   x
```

and person number #2 could strike:

```
1  1  1
x  x  x
```

In this way one learns that there are many basic patterns that can be effectively divided between people and instruments to create an interesting linguistic percussive conversation. Feel free to reverse the hands when you have a left handed student.

Here is a possible configuration for 12 people, two in each group. The patterns can be clapped first. When you look at this chart you'll probably realize that it is imperative that each person be able to identify the downbeat. This is what you have been working toward with the simpler exercises that have been taught at the beginning of the session. Instrument possibilities are: Native American bass drums, congas, agogo bells, claves, percussion tubes, bongos (see page 101).

```
#1    1 1  1 1  1 1  1 1
      x    x    x    x

#2    1 1  1 1  1 1  1 1
      x    x x  x    x x

#3    1 1  1 1  1 1  1 1  1 1  1 1  1 1  1 1
      x      x  x         x      x  x

#4    1 1  1 1  1 1  1 1
        x    x    x    x

#5    1 1  1 1  1 1  1 1
      x    x    xx

#6    1 1  1 1  1 1  1 1  1 1  1 1  1 1  1 1
                xx   xx             xx   xx
```

The first pattern is drawn from Nigerian roots. The second pattern, the bell pattern, is Afro-Cuban. The patterns are broken up and simplified at the beginning and gain in complexity as the musician matures. This kind of group musical activity provides a contrast with the solo piano experience allowing yet another venue for musical expression, musical ideas and musical communication (not to mention FUN!).

During piano lessons a student will sometimes look longingly at the instruments asking me if she can have some time with them.

"You bet," I say. "Finish your piece and let's play for awhile on the drums."

This is a valuable musical interlude and broadens the students' horizons. Respect for other cultures is paramount in The Sheli Nan Method. Adherence to the spontaneity of the musical experience and the integrity of the mission surpasses in fun and learning ability a purely linear musical approach such as following only a schedule and a book. As a student begins to understand what to do on the percussion instruments, then the fun of improvisation begins. What exactly is required when playing the percussion instruments? Besides learning the patterns, it is essential to listen, to cooperate, to know when to come in, and to be respectful of the instruments and one another. In fact, all of the essential ingredients that make up a functioning community take place right at the moment the woven basket with the gaily colored instruments is taken out.

A guided improvisation can go something like this:

"We are in the jungle. It is early morning. The birds are just beginning to awaken (rainsticks, little bells etc.). Soon the sun is up and the animals are prowling (all instruments played moderately). Wait a minute! There's a chase! The lion is after the zebra! (Drums come in using mallets and hands.) The jungle is in an uproar. (All play fast and furiously.) That was close. The zebra got away. (Dynamics - the sound comes down.) It is starting to get dark. (Larger instruments drop out.) The animals are getting ready to sleep. (Quieter still.) The only sound left is the wind in the trees (rainsticks)."

An unguided improvisation could consist of the following: playing in a sensitive way with others, thinking dynamics, playing band (a big favorite at this studio) with guitars and drums and singing and dancing.

Teacher always plays too. Hey, this is fun. You want to improvise and listen for your beautiful sound as well. Teach by example. Always. Take part in these musical rituals. Show the kids when you have come up with something that excites you. If you can play guitar do that too! Encourage people to sing in open improvisations, and to dance. Sometimes play the congas and let the youngsters, just to feel the joy of the rhythmic pulse, dance. This is about musical freedom. And the joy of it all!

IMPROVISATION

Next course on the menu is "MAKE SOMETHING UP". This is the moment of trust. How very exciting to place one's fingers on the keys and create. There are structured improvisations and unstructured improvisations. In an unstructured improvisation I ask the student, regardless of age, to listen to himself and to give me a good ending. Once that has been accomplished I talk about mood. If the student has arrived at the studio feeling upset I ask him to make something up that uses that feeling.

"You seem kind of upset today. Make up something sad for me. You can use the pedal. Just put your fingers on the keys and let them choreograph themselves. [For kids say, "Just let your fingers dance around."] I don't want you to think. I want you to listen. I'm not even going to look at you. I'm just going to listen. Use the pedal if you want."

This is a very powerful experience for the student. It can be a very powerful experience for the teacher as well. Here we have a non-judgmental moment at the keyboard. What a relief. The student tentatively plays. Teacher listens. Soon both are lost in an original world of sound. Adults are more self-conscious than children and still yearn for this experience. Teacher becomes the chronicler of the interior event. "I am moved," I say.

Sometimes the younger students want a story before they make something up. Sometimes a story goes on for a number of weeks. As the student becomes comfortable with the process, the amount of information expands.

This is the order in which I teach improvisation and composition. Once again, there is never any rush. Let's say the student is a little older, 9 years old perhaps.

She has come into class having composed a little melody in the right hand. First ask her to play the melody through three times. In this way you ascertain if the melody is *set.* (Repeated the same way each time.) When it is set, ask her to play the melody in *unison.* (Both hands at the same time, same notes.) When she can do that ask her to play a chord in the left hand. Help her find a chord that fits her melody. After she can play the melody in the right hand, with the chord in the left hand, ask her to play the melody in the left hand and the chord in the right hand. Now ask her to play the melody in the right hand and the chord in the left hand three times in the first octave she has played it in. Then ask her to do the same thing up an octave. Then ask her to return to the original octave. Talk to her about ABA.

"Pieces frequently end just like they start. Twinkle Twinkle Little Star is a perfect example. Do you see how the first section of Twinkle Twinkle Little Star repeats at the end? If we call the first section A, then we can call the second section B. Then we go back to A to end it."

The same is true of the little piece that is taking shape under her fingers. In the first octave we are calling the section A. In the second octave we are calling the section B and when she returns to the first octave call the section A. If she understands this you can go on.

"For next week, instead of having the B section an octave up, why don't you make something up that is different, (contrasting) to what you have made up so far? For instance, you could do a series of chords. This could be the new B section. It would be really different than the A section."

When the student has come in with two contrasting sections to her piece, it is time to teach her how to put it in minor. Teach her that the third note of the scale, the second note of the arpeggio, is flatted and that this produces the minor sound. Now she has a further choice. She can play the A section in major. She can go into the B section in minor, and return to the A section in major. There is a good chance that she won't want to do any of this. That is okay. The idea is to give her as many choices as possible. Rarely critique the piece aesthetically. To teach improvisation and composition effectively is to give the structural tools so that the composer on her own can make the aesthetic decisions. It is not up to the teacher to critique the sound. It is more supportive and educational to make structural suggestions.

If the student understands ABA form, and how to place her melody in major and minor, she can be taught to identify the tonic (I), which is the chord built on the first note of the scale. Then she can learn the subdominant (IV) built on the fourth note of the scale, and the dominant (V), the chord built on the fifth note of the scale. This gives the student further tools for her improvisations.

You also are beginning to teach the basic tenets of theory. Begin in the key of C. Have the student play the tonic in both hands. (CEG) Then have the student stay with the chord in the left hand and using only the three chord notes in the right hand, play them in any order for as long as he wants. After explaining to him how to play the subdominant, (FAC), do the same there. Have the left hand play the subdominant chord and have the right hand play those three notes in any combo with any rhythm. Repeat this for the dominant. (GBD) Then either leave them with this pattern

I IV V I

or elaborate on it. For instance:

I IV V IV I

Tell the student that this is the basis of rock and roll. People love this!

For homework the student uses the pattern playing the chords in the left hand and the notes in the right hand. Each week this simple pattern can become more complex. The variations are endless. Soon the student recognizes that he can add notes other than the notes of the chord. Then the pattern can be extended or changed, such as transposing it into a minor key or into another key altogether.

Teach the circle of fifths as a compositional tool. For less advanced students the first four chords can be learned and improvised on (C-G-D-A). For more advanced students the entire circle provides theoretical information and musical ideas.

Improvisation is psychic release time. The student gets to do whatever he wants to do. The three main ingredients for a valuable improvisation are:

1. Listen to yourself
2. Create a good ending
3. Go with a mood (or moods).

As the student becomes more advanced compositions begin to take shape. One's own natural rhythm emerges. The student comes to class with a musical fragment that she has memorized from an improvisational moment at home. Listen to this fragment. Have her play it in unison. Now play it with a chord. Switch hands. Play it in minor. Play it in the dominant. Now there are many musical ideas for the student to consider. The fragment may be the beginning of a piece. It may be the middle. It may be just a starting point for an entirely new dialogue. As time goes on the piece is crafted. ABA form has been introduced. The crafting of a piece can take more than a month.

The organic experience of composing comes before the piece is written out. Composition comes from inside out. When the student is comfortable with the written language of music, the process of writing out the piece can begin. If the writing of the music comes before or at the same time as the composing, the student will be severely limited by what she is writing down. Many beginning students compose pieces of great complexity and beauty. If they were limited by their writing abilities, the pieces would not have the scope and depth they often do.

If the student has been composing steadily for some years, and has now become accustomed to the written musical language, it is fine to begin writing out his piece. Have him begin by writing out the melody. Get the notes on paper for both hands. Frequently the time signature can be the most problematic. Ask the student to lightly draw in where he thinks the measures should go. (Always in pencil!!) Help him to figure out the time signature of the piece by reducing all beats to the smallest value possible. Figure out where the notes correspond to the beats. (Percussion training will be a great help here.) Once this has been done teach him to draw a technical map of the piece. Figure out the key signature. Place the tonic sign under (I) the tonic chords. See if he can find the subdominant and the dominant. Sometimes there will be jazz voicings. Figure these out using a jazz chord chart that can be bought at your local music store. Listen to him play the piece and help him identify where the dynamics are and what they should be.

This part of the journey in composition is reserved for the serious talented student. It is too difficult for most people. You will know when you have a student that is motivated to follow this path. You will want to do everything in your power to assist him on his journey.

Improvisation is a breath of fresh air both in practice and during a lesson. It is a spiritually soothing non-linear moment when, after intense concentration, it is delightful to let the fingers traverse the keys in any direction they choose to go. The act of listening non-judgmentally allows one to hear all sorts of sounds beautiful and dissonant, that are an end in themselves.

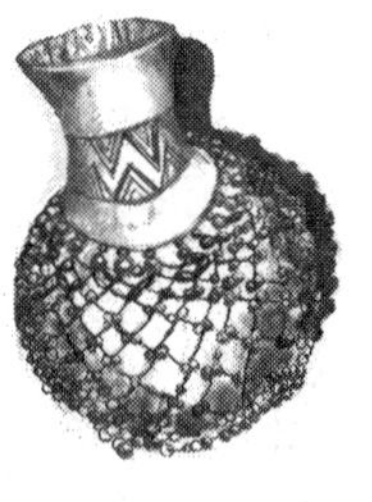

PRACTICE

THE ART OF PRACTICE

When I sit down to practice a sense of relief comes to me. I am reconnecting with my language—a physical heartfelt experience. I know a moment of divinity when my fingers rush across the keyboard and I feel elevated enlightened and lucky to be once more on the musical route. I am carried by the buoyant Musical Spirit—The Muse. She encourages me, teases me, and supports me in my quest.

When I sit down to practice I am realizing my obligation. I am crossing yet another thing off my list. I am taking my educational vitamins. I am forcing myself to engage in a minute precarious difficult task.

When I sit down to practice I am once again student. And it can be so frustrating.

When I was a child I used to throw my books on the floor and stamp on them. I raged, tears in my eyes, when I couldn't do my piece. I felt personally insulted and infuriated. This basic facet of my character gave me the strength to engage the Muse head on.

"Oh, so you think I can't do that, do you?" I was forever getting better just to show "them" whoever "they" were.

I was and am engaged in a contest with myself. I strive to grow, to encompass new material. I WANT THAT. Whatever that is; be it baroque music with it's persnickety precision, or a new piece that I am composing. I want desperately, anxiously, importantly and immediately to understand. And yet, practice is an ongoing state of mind. Very very occasionally is it immediate. It would be more appropriate to say that the struggle is long term, very long term, as in life-time long term.

When I sit down to practice, in a deep nonverbal way, I am affirming myself. I have to like myself, and be willing to engage and entertain myself with my struggle and my growth. I enter into an agreement and dialog with myself.

Some days I get up from the keyboard and I am exhilarated. What I have worked so hard to achieve has begun to make musical sense to me. I have practiced, crying, with the beauty I have touched. The glorious sound, ringing from my instrument, has reached me and I have been generously given a moment of pure spiritual beauty embodied in an acoustic physical and emotional musical phrase. I have been part of this grand plan —the composer, the instrument, the performer (student, teacher), the Muse.

Some days I get up from my practice and I am depressed. I did not play well. I did not get the effect. I felt leaden. My fingers would not obey. I went through the motions, music did not result. I ponder my life. I ponder my future. This mood lasts approximately 3 hours. Then once more fortified with energy and optimism, hope and desire, I am ready to practice again.

Sometimes one feels disconnected and out of sorts. It is important to practice all the same. This is especially true for the beginner. Nothing comes for free in the learning of music. (Unless you are Mozart and an argument can be made that he paid a price in a different way.) It is a difficult constant path leading ever onward and upward. We by our very fortitude, earn the spiritual delight that comes our way. When we practice, we are in effect paying obeisance to the Muse. When we have gone through the motions enough times, we begin, through our physical consciousness and physical flexibility, to be worthy of a profound moment that touches us and elevates us as only genius can.

This type of experience is an important aspect in the process of teaching a student how to practice. The adult student, by virtue of the fact that she is paying for the lesson with her own money, is apt to practice just so that she can get her money's worth. This is admirable. Couple this practicality with the above sentiments and there is fertile ground for learning.

The musical experience conjures up every emotion in the book! We all know that doing something that has to be done is hard work. And we resist. So it is advisable to use everything at your disposal in order to assist the student in realizing a truly fulfilling musical experience. Sympathy, encouragement, and enjoyment begin the process. (Enjoyment for the teacher. When we make it clear that listening to our students is a great joy for us, we are participating in their private ritual and we become privy to a most intimate and exciting moment in their lives. They also feel great!)

When the occasion merits, ask the parents to help remind the student to practice. A practice schedule can be devised that works with the other activities in the student's life. The student can be asked to sit down each day and do each piece 3 times, and/or practice for 5 minutes through 1 hour depending on the level. Setting a schedule is a good idea.

For the child, an excellent way to structure his schedule is to take a daily activity, like dinner, and have practice time be right afterwards. This makes it easy to remember and practice time becomes integrated into the family consciousness. It is delightful to hear a child practice when one is in the kitchen after dinner. This is a lovely way to bring the parents into the process. Tell the parent to support the child by giving him a compliment now and then and letting him know how hard they think the piece is and how proud they are of the child's progress.

Practice is essential 5 out of 7 days weekly. It does not have to be for long. Most people do not become professional musicians. Therefore the constant application of musical education can be taken daily in small doses. It will become clear to student and teacher which person is particularly attracted to music. Then the schedule adjusts according to the practice load. This is a natural progression and should not be forced. Stress listening over and over again. During practice tell your students to listen to themselves play. Just playing the right notes is not enough. Being able to execute difficult "small motor" challenges is a physical thrill. When students are able to successfully overcome these physical challenges—while listening to themselves in the process—the experience is especially gratifying.

Next come scales and arpeggios. Scales and arpeggios are our building blocks. They are the body trainers of our fingers. All athletes must have a discipline, or rather, a warm-up. All sports have technique. A gymnast must constantly do a variety of exercises like sit-ups and stretches to maintain her flexibility. A baseball player has to run and play catch before he goes out on the field. These are some of the examples I use with my students when I teach them about scales and arpeggios. This technique of ours, in a very precise and time conscious way, builds discipline into our hands. Sometimes I tell my kids that they are the parent and their hands are the kids.

"Now make those kids behave," I say. "Each finger has to do just what you want it to do. If the fourth finger needs to play that D, you can make it do it."

The kids love this analogy. Scales and arpeggios become something to brag about, as in, "I got a new arpeggio today."

Rather than being experienced as a dry and uneventful necessity, my students love their scales and arpeggios and feel empowered by them. With the little kids, in private lessons, begin with one or two scales. If they are comfortable extend this somewhat.

With the older students they learn the major scales and arpeggios, then the minors, the dominant 7ths and the diminished scales and arpeggios. I rarely need to speak to my teenage students about practice because when they have gotten to a certain age and have spent a certain amount of time with me, they know what my expectations are, and even more exciting, they know what they are able to do.

Even the very difficult music becomes a stimulating and exciting game. What we are talking about here is the joy of learning. Please remember that. Practice is about the joy of learning. Put it in the right context, and you will be off to a great start with your students!

When someone comes to me that has not practiced for two consecutive weeks, (and this happens at times with all ages but more so with 7-8 year olds, teenagers, and adults) I say, "Fine. Guess what we are going to do today?" I then take the student through the structure of a practice time. We do our scales and arpeggios. Then we get to a piece, usually Czerny, and we do the right hand alone three times. Then we do the left hand alone three times. Then we do it hands together three times.

Generally by now the student is inwardly fuming. If it is an adult, his thinking goes something like this, "I'm paying all this money so she can hear me practice?"

If it is a kid, the feeling most often verbalized is, "Do I have to?"

As they well know, the answer is invariably, "YES," followed by, "And what exactly are we doing now? Do you know what this is called?"

A roll of the eyes and the child answers, "Practice".

"You got it," I reply. "Do you understand how I want you to do it now?"

Frequently it does not take more than two or three times for this to occur before the student gets the picture!

When a student sits down to practice and opens the book in front of him, he must always know which note the piece is starting on. He must be able to identify the sharp or flat and the key signature if he is old enough. Depending on age, the time signature is also taken into account. For little kids say, "Always know the note the piece starts on and ends on. Always know if there is a black note, and which one. Figure out which scale goes with which black note. This means we are playing around with the notes of that scale. It also gives us clues as to our position on the keyboard."

Practice is the accumulation of knowledge. The process is amazing because if the student does just a little bit of practicing daily, at the end of the week the piece has improved. The progress is not noticeable from day to day. It is noticeable by the time the student has gotten to her lesson. This is a concept that is learned by one's own personal experience. We can speak about it to our students and then they can go home and learn it for themselves.

Learning to play the piano can be frustrating, both for students who practice and students who don't. And that is the way it goes. The musical path is not easy. And so what? The pleasure comes in being able to do something hard and do it well. And the work required to complete the project becomes a badge of accomplishment when music is created.

There are many ways to structure practice. Here is another example.When the child is little I ask him to play everything three times at home five days a week. This works better than assigning a time, like 10 minutes, because it is easier for a small person to quantify time this way, rather than by a clock. It also gives him independence and responsibility and keeps the parent out of the arrangement.

When a person is older, if they need help with structuring practice time, I ask for a specific amount of time depending on their age, music and commitment.

In my experience, an excellent practice technique for more complex pieces is that of DOUBLING THE VOICES. As each side of our brain controls the opposite hand, when we double the voices we are giving information to the other side of our brain. What this literally means is that we play the treble clef in both hands at the same time. The fingering for the left hand makes no difference at all. Then we play the bass clef in both hands at the same time. The fingering for the right hand makes no difference. Then we play the hands again in their original positions and the information has transferred itself into new cranial areas and the understanding of the piece is enhanced.

TROUBLE SPOTS. Some measures are consistent stumbling blocks. Most of the time this is due to some combination of uncomfortable and impractical fingering. These measures are called trouble spots. An effective technique for dealing with trouble spots is to thoroughly relearn them with more practical fingering and a better understanding of how that fingering helps to achieve the desired effect. Depending on the difficulty, the voices can be doubled in this instance as well. If the fingering is well understood and still the measure causes difficulty, it should be memorized so that the student is freed up from having to look at the music.

The METRONOME* is a marvelous tool to assist us in our playing. It is not the definitive word on how a piece should be played. It is only a tool to be used with beginning and intermediate students sparingly. For more advanced students it can be fun. If a student is playing a piece and changing tempi through-out the piece, doing it with a metronome will set him straight immediately because he will be able to see where he goes off. When use of the metronome is taught in this context it becomes a valuable listening device for rhythmic correction.

It is important to remember that the metronome was invented toward the end of Beethoven's life. There is a chance he could not even hear it, although he certainly could see it and extrapolate its sound. It is not important to set tempi (generally) for the student. The student can take the most difficult section of the piece and begin the metronome setting for the entire piece at that speed. When the trouble spot has been learned, the speed can be increased. It is not necessary to use the metronome daily. It is interesting to use the metronome, particularly when one is desirous of more speed, accuracy and clarity of sound.

MEMORY: When we ask our students to memorize a piece we are stretching them in more ways than one. Engaging the memory is another way of learning in a musical context. The student is exercising her mental muscles memorizing pieces. Memory allows us to learn something new. Scientists know little about what happens in the brain when it stores memories. However, they are almost certain that storing new memories involves chemical changes in the nerve cells of the brain where the higher brain functions reside, such as the use of language. The more thoroughly we engage the sensory apparatus - through the tactile, visual, aural, and emotional aspects of the music - the more profound and fulfilling our experience and learning will be.

There is sensual memory that takes place in the fingers. There is visual memory. There is aural memory. There is emotional memory. This is another example of how we engage the whole organism in the pursuit of the musical experience.

In practice, and during the lesson, it is important to remind the student to breathe. We have a tendency to hold our breath when we come to difficult passages. Learning to breathe at the keyboard frees up physical and psychic energy that can then flow toward the piece. It is the most basic training and it is so often overlooked. When a student holds her breath, she becomes uncomfortable and tense. With the steady breathing required for this physical activity, the sound is enhanced and the student feels more peaceful and focused on the task.

Before a student gathering or a performance of some kind, when the mastery of the piece must be the very best the student is capable of, the piece can be practiced by playing the last line first. Once this is done a number of times, the last page of the piece can be practiced. Then the student goes back to the beginning to practice the piece.

This is a solid practice structure. Do all the scales and arpeggios once through. Then comes Czerny. After Czerny improvise for awhile. Then go to the pieces. Start with the baroque pieces and work forward chronologically. Utilize the techniques discussed above for the more difficult pieces. Take time to think, listen and relax. Practice becomes a meditation.

CZERNY

There is something eternal about Czerny. He epitomizes the classical period so thoroughly and teaches us it's language with so much generosity.

Carl Czerny was born in Vienna in 1791. His father, Wenzel Czerny, was a piano teacher. Wenzel Czerny taught his little son well. Carl, by the time he was ten years old, was playing Clementi, Mozart, and other well known composers of the time. Due to his good musical memory and the constant influence of his father and his father's musical friends, Carl had memorized everything he had learned.

He first met Beethoven when he was 10 years old. His father's friends convinced his father to take Carl to Beethoven to see if he would teach him. Czerny was rather nervous when he arrived at Beethoven's upstairs flat. When they went into the room it was a mess. There was music everywhere. There were a number of men standing around talking. Beethoven looked kind of frightening. He had great yellowed wads of cotton sticking out of both of his ears.(He was not deaf yet.) Carl unobtrusively slipped onto the piano bench and began playing.

He was too frightened to play any of Beethoven's (the Master's) music. Finally, after about 20 minutes, Beethoven said, "Can't you play anything of mine?" Carl had memorized everything he had learned by Beethoven. He began to play. Beethoven was interested and he listened. Then he sat down on the bench with Carl and they began to play the Sonata Pathetique together. Imagine that scene for a moment. Thus began a relationship that lasted the rest of Beethoven's life!

Beethoven sent Carl home that day telling his father to make sure he got "Emanuel Bach's treatise of The True Art of Keyboard Playing." In the first lesson Beethoven had Carl concentrate exclusively on scales in all keys. He showed him the correct position of the hands and fingers. This was unknown to most players at that time.

Then Beethoven taught Carl the practice pieces in Bach's treatise. He made Czerny particularly aware of the "legato" which other pianists at the time still considered unfeasible at the fortepiano. "Choppy and smartly detached playing was still in favor then as it had been in Mozart's time!" (see page 117.)

Beethoven told Czerny in later years that he had heard Mozart play several times. Because the fortepiano was in it's infancy then, Mozart had acquired a manner of playing on the spinet (harpsichord) that was more common to that instrument and in no way suited to the fortepiano.

Nowadays we know that this last statement was not entirely correct. In fact, the early fortepianos were more like harpsichords with hammers. As a result of this, Mozart played his pieces both with articulation and with dynamics in order to get the most that he could out of his instrument.

Carl Czerny was so fortunate. He could play everything Beethoven wrote with clarity, musicality and by memory. Until the end of Beethoven's life, the great composer was well disposed toward Czerny and treated him in a friendly way.

But what to do about Czerny's deep abiding need to compose? Imagine how difficult that was when Beethoven, one of the greatest minds of our time, was his teacher! Nothing he could compose would ever measure up to his teacher.Not to be deterred though, he decided to write a course of exercises that encompassed every aspect of the musical experience to date. He wrote exercises for the left hand, for the right hand, for crossing hands, for lyricism, for speed, for arpeggios etc.

His very generosity has been a beacon for music students everywhere. His books are a dictionary of the "Classical language". Composer he was and composer he is.

Perhaps Czerny's works do not always move us in depth, the way great music moves us. But then again, here is the chance to play more on the analytical side. We can be moved by Czerny, but we can also suspend emotional commitment, listen to his teaching, and enjoy the process of strengthening our fingers in the classical language.

Czerny became a composer, teacher and pianist. By the age of fifteen his teaching career was legendary. He taught Franz Liszt. He composed more than 1000 works for almost every vocal and instrumental form. He also arranged many works by other composers for piano. But he is known for his Studies and this is the way he has inserted himself into the great time line of musical history. Every great pianist has played Czerny. When your student practices Czerny, he is becoming a part of the great stream of musical consciousness in the development of keyboard music.

Each book of exercises is dedicated to a certain aspect of musical grammar. Czerny is challenging, rewarding, and irritating. We have a standing joke amongst my students, young and old. Every Czerny piece has its irritation quotient. He has bequeathed us a great gift. When he is taught from this perspective, a combination of our compassion for him, and our gratitude for his "musical dictionary", the learning takes on a new dimension of joy and fun!

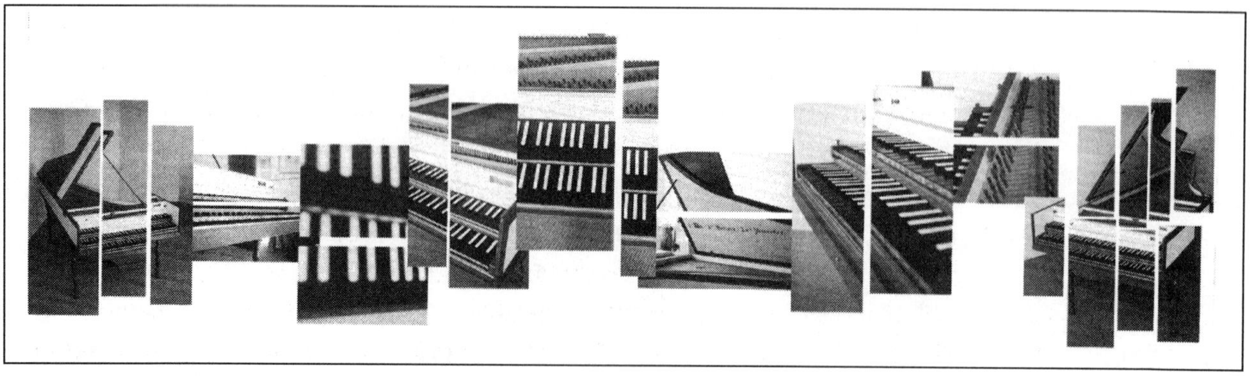

HOW TO BE HIP

HIP stands for Historically Informed Performance. In order to understand how to be Hip, it is important to understand the history of Western (keyboard) Music. The development of keyboard music began 500 years ago. The instruments of that time were the virginal*,the clavichord, variations of these two basic instruments, and the harpsichord which occupied center stage from 1570 - 1790.

The original harpsichords were "mechanized" string instruments. The lute, a precursor to the modern day guitar, served as the model. When the key of the harpsichord is gently pressed a small rod call called a jack* pops up. On the edge of the jack is a tiny piece of plastic which is called a tongue. A small piece called the plectrum sticks out and hits the string, plucking it. In the past the jack was made of wood and the plectrum from quill. Nowadays, the jack the tongue and the plectrum are usually made from plastic.

The strength used in striking the key makes no difference to the dynamics of forte and piano. The main way one has of increasing and diminishing the keyboard sound, in addition to articulation, is by the coupling and uncoupling of the strings.The harpsichord has 1, 2 and 3 sets of strings depending on the model played. For this discussion we will use a French double manual harpsichord as our reference.

This is a harpsichord with 2 concurrent keyboards, or manuals. The top manual has one set of strings and the bottom manual has another set of strings both measuring 8'. There is another set of strings that can be coupled and uncoupled depending on the piece played, and these measure 4'. There is also a "buff" that muffles one set of single strings to produce a "lute-like" sound. Most harpsichords have levers and/or knobs, and occasionally knee pedals, to work the strings. When the strings are coupled the sound is louder. When the strings are uncoupled the sound is quieter. But how can you make anything sound different on the harpsichord without the accustomed forte and piano? Won't all of the music always sound the same?

For a pianist coming to the harpsichord for the first time, the instrument may seem to offer little potential for nuance and expression, especially in terms of the dynamic range of the modern piano. When one begins to study this marvelous instrument there is a vast world of subtle intricate dynamic revelation known as articulation.

Articulation is literally defined as the amount of space between the notes. This can be accomplished with variations. A rhythmic alteration can be created when the left hand is played straight or strict, and the right hand is played crooked or free. There is also the practice of over dotting (inegal). Frequently the decisions to articulate are based on the harmonic modulations, the bar-lines, and the character of the piece. If a dance tune is being played, the piece would have to reflect the rhythm of the dance.

The 18th century musical concept was based on design rather than melody. Because the instrument did not differentiate dynamically the way the modern piano does, it was common for two musical lines to play against one another, both with the same depth and integrity (counterpoint*). There was no harmonic division of melody and accompaniment. The left hand proudly took its course with the same strength and clarity as the right hand. As a result, it is extremely important to articulate either at the bar-lines, or perhaps every two measures depending on a harmony change. (Weak beats versus strong beats.)

Anyone who has played advanced Bach on the piano has had the perplexing experience of wondering, "Whatever am I doing?"

When we understand the workings of the instrument Bach and his fellow baroque composers composed for, we understand what the parameters of the music were and how the instrument, along with the culture, religion and mores of familial life, contributed to the design concept of this age.

Preceding melody and accompaniment, we have a rigorous and magnificent musical conversation taking place in both hands, frequently with 2,3,4 or even 5 voices. These voices seem to be speaking all at once. The sheer numbers of notes coming from a Bach fugue leave us senseless and fatigued. How do we make sense of it all?

The answer, in a word, is articulation. Articulation predates the concept of phrasing. We are taught how the architecture of the piece is conceived by examining each voice within the piece and deciding via strong and weak beats, harmonic changes, the key of the piece, and the meter, where to articulate.

Once the piece has been mapped out, (see page 72) we have an understanding of the articulation required.There are many different gradations of articulation; large, small, quick, hesitant, sad, joyous. We look to the key signature. We look to the character of the piece.

Begin to articulate with one voice. Then add the other voices. The design of the piece will become apparent. When this lengthy process is complete practice the piece voice by voice, slowly. There is nothing more challenging than playing a Bach fugue, with appropriate articulation, in each voice.

The architecture of the piece has been revealed to us. We now have control of the design. We are able to enter the great expanse of sound the composer has given us, and marvel at the vaulted ceilings and the crenelated walls.

We do not walk out of a cathedral humming a little ditty. We come away with a sense of humanity's achievements, and with a sense of towering magnitude, depth and clarity.

Try playing a Bach fugue without articulation. It will probably sound muddy and dense. Put it on a piano, using pedal and heavy going dynamics. At once, the clarity is lost, the joy reduced to a grinding senseless exercise going nowhere.

Most of us learned Bach from poorly edited editions. Editors tried desperately to appropriate Bach for modern day piano having no idea of the style of playing common to the 18th century. Phrasing was added. Dynamics were added. There was a tendency to highlight the first fugue theme whenever and wherever it appeared and to ignore all that went after it.The folly of this approach is that the brilliant Old Master's voice was lost in a 19 century miasma of thickened sensibility.

We now know that all slurs until 1880 are articulation, not staccato and legato. There is no way to notate super legato which on the harpsichord means that you are holding down as many of the notes as possible. The minuet on page 72 has been notated two different ways. Each example of notation has the same meaning. The first way uses a slash to remind the student where to separate the voices. The second way uses our current notation to enhance a baroque interpretation of the piece. Hence, a staccato is not a staccato. It is an indication of an articulated note. A slur is not a phrase. It indicates super legato.

We now have the possibility of learning the original musical vision of Bach. This takes place with an excellent urtext edition, (see page 109) and a teacher who can teach us how to be HIP. If we are fortunate enough we can learn to play harpsichord. If we understand this teaching, it is possible to elaborate Bach on the modern piano. After all, most people don't have harpsichords.

Getting a harpsichord has become much easier and if you shop carefully there is a vast price range. Please get some consultations with a harpsichord teacher and learn the baroque language for the instrument that spoke it. Then your teaching will be enhanced and completed by this information.

The truth is that Bach sounds marvelous on any instrument. Played competently and with an understanding of the style and content of the period, Bach and his fellow composers can be taken onto any instrument with success. One now understands the context for each different period of music.

Consider your piano for one moment. When you lean toward it with power in your curved arms, and you press the keys with strength, the sound swells and the listener is borne on strong tides of musical vibrations.

The experience is vastly different on the harpsichord. It is extremely satisfying to produce the quantity of emotion at the harpsichord with the use of a technique *specific* to the harpsichord, that is produced at the piano. The piano and harpsichord, although different, share a keyboard in common. The literature that developed for these instruments has been informed by the structure of the instruments. Human beings bring the same diligence, excitement, talent and depth to each keyboard.

Each composer has a vision. This is a conscious musical idea that encompasses the structure of the piece, the notes, harmonies and melodies, the texture and the meter. The limits and abilities of the human body are inherent to the parameters of the design. Whatever the instrument size shape and form, the music, the composer and the design concept will be affected.

If a person is not familiar with the harpsichord, its beauty and to the modern mind, its irregularities, then the vision that Bach set forth will not be intact. The beauty of the musical discourse has to do with how our great Masters say what they say. And although they all speak of the same subjects, they do so in their own styles!

The harpsichord is a light instrument suited for small performance venues. A salon setting is perfect. Imagine yourself in somebody's home. In the lovely living room a small group of people has gathered to listen. The instrument, painted beautifully, sits quietly awaiting the moment it will get to sing. The audience is excited and before the concert begins everybody gets very quiet. The performer must be intimately in touch with his instrument in order to draw forth emotive dynamics. The passion of the music does not depend on the loudness of a particular instrument.

It is clear that the composers whom we recognize as the greatest of the baroque and classical periods generously left for us their great philosophical musings in the form of music. All events momentous to humankind are included in the great libraries of classics that Bach, Mozart, Beethoven, Chopin, Schubert and Schumann and many others have given to us. This is our musical heritage.

By the turn of the 19th century a playable version of the fortepiano, a much lighter precursor to the contemporary piano, had arrived. There actually had been earlier pianos but they did not survive because the playing mechanisms had not been perfected. The keyboard instrument was in a constant state of development.

This slighter, lighter edition of the earliest piano, by the turn of the century, was being produced in greater volumes. More people had access to it. After reigning for 200 years, the harpsichord was beginning to be considered old fashioned. With the new instrument came new composers.

Mozart, born in 1756, composed his first published work, Minuet in E, Kochel 5, at age 6. Soon thereafter he also learned of the recently developed fortepiano due to his touring as a wunderkind.

If we understand Mozart's world, where dynamics were created on his first keyboard instrument by articulation, a very differing touch technique, and the concept of design as the basis of melodic material, then the interpretation of his music acquires new significance. We can then recognize how Mozart's ideas and works eventually evolved beyond the musical conventions and limits of his time.

As a young composer newly arrived in Vienna, Beethoven met Mozart who said of him, "That young fellow has a lot of talent."

As Mozart took us from the baroque era into the classical era, Beethoven took the musical tradition yet a step further and added his own voice to the musical weave that is our cultural heritage. We have seen moments of Bach shine in him, we hear our own hearts beating rapidly with his pulse. We have listened to moments of agonizing beauty that remind us of Mozart. Beethoven pushed the boundaries of classical form and harmony.

Chopin was born in 1810. And by the time he was a teenager we had the most modern precursor to the piano of today. The wood was heavier and the instrument was double stringed. Chopin was a student of Bach and utilized counterpoint and conceptual design to great effect. He was lyrical and graceful, reminiscent of Mozart. He was passionate and insistent like Beethoven. And his unique voice, along with his unique instrument, became a haunting over arching melody like a ribbon flowing above a vast construct. His hands were large. As the piano progressed the compass of an octave grew much larger.The keys of the harpsichord are small. The key dip of the harpsichord is shallow. Everything is closer.

The keys of the piano, in comparison, were so much larger by the 1820s. The music began to be written for larger hands that more easily accommodated this new keyboard.

A new style, an expansive style of composition, arrived, partly because of the breadth of the new keyboard, and mostly because the sound could now be sustained. There were pedals! A large sound could be sustained for a long time. The decay on the harpsichord was rapid. The decay on the piano lasted a long time. More people could hear it because larger concert halls could accommodate larger audiences. In these more expansive venues, the performance became more removed from the audience. And the performer was now more removed from the audience. What had been an intimate experience between performer and audience in the baroque period, became a more formal experience socially.

Dussek, the Bohemian composer, was the first performer to turn the piano sideways. In that way his profile could be seen and the audience could get a more intense experience of the performance. In baroque times this was not necessary because everyone was up close. Sometimes real close!

The Bach-Abel concert series that took place in London in 1768, was one of the first musical series open to a paying public. As concert music became more accessible to a growing middle class of merchants and businessmen, more people were able to afford to participate both in ownership of instruments and attendance at concerts. The Bach-Abel concert series presented a fortepiano on stage for the first time along with the more familiar harpsichord.

The rules were expanding. What had been appropriate during the baroque period was now no longer so. Composers were again writing Fantasies, pieces that had different sections that explored different moods. There was a shift away from form. During the romantic period the music became more descriptive. Schumann wrote "Forest Scenes' and the listener felt as though he were in the forest. As the rules expanded, it became impossible for the performer to do what was once considered the best of form, improvise on the music. Adherence to the written score became imperative because recognizable rules were no longer followed. In order to portray the composer's vision, the notes had to be played exactly as written. All ornaments were now notated. The music became more detailed in embellishment. Over a period of time composers have been more and more adamant about their music being performed exactly as written. This may be due to an excess of individualism that has taken away from the composers' work.

This history and analysis is essential in teaching us how to play what we play. A teacher must be versed in historically informed performance in order to successfully teach the musical language. This language is a multi-dexterous one with its own grammatical rules. Unlike old English, and other archaic languages, we still speak this one in the form in which it was codified two centuries ago. We strive to speak the musical language in its original format so that we can be respectful of the messenger and sure of getting the message. As in Bach, for instance. We want to get every possible piece of information that was left to us. This man had a lot to say about everything.

Once we understand the harpsichord, it is possible to transfer Bach onto the modern piano. We can even take advantage of the pedal but only if we understand articulation and the style of baroque playing. Then the decisions we make as we traverse history from harpsichord to the modern piano will be in keeping with the musical visions of Bach and the other Great Masters.

TEACHER CONSIDERATIONS

PARENTS

Parents to be on the lookout to avoid:

Every instructor can probably tell you horror stories about the parents of students. Is it possible to come up with a "parent profile" that helps us identify which families we would enjoy working with, and which families we would be able to contribute to? I use the word "families" purposefully because when a child studies seriously with a teacher, that person becomes more important for the child than for the parents. It is inadvisable to teach a child without taking into account the student's home environment. The parents who pay the bills and generally strive to support and encourage their children are a vital part of the equation. Teachers need to be able to speak to parents and to educate them about the study of music and what it entails.

The largest obstacles we face when dealing with parents are their expectations which are often misguided. The study of piano is life long. The rewards can be great, but to get these rewards we need to work a lot, practice, study and think about the material. The true engagement is not one of "product" but one of "process".

If we view the musical experience solely in goal oriented terms, we miss out on the learning that takes place along the way. Yes, the piece and the way it is played are ultimately very important. We all have goals that we strive for. However, in the musical world, these goals are long term.

If a student's parent wants immediate progress, it is important to tell this parent up front that the process does not really work that way. The child is learning how to connect with herself in a creative way. Besides learning how to coordinate her fingers with the visual imagery, she is also learning how to listen, and how to be creative. This is a remarkable process that fills one with joy. The joy comes from the creativity, the stimulation and the difficulty. And the joy comes from the sound and the student's growing ability to learn this language, connect with a vast world of musical literature, and become musically literate herself.

This may be a lot to explain. The essential, however, is that the parents must understand from the start that when the child learns how to play a piece, although that constitutes an accomplishment, it is only a small step into the world of music. And it is not quantifiable. Some people need a lot more time than others to learn the same material. There is no standardized musical test. The beauty of this discipline is that all are free to learn at their own speed. If you get a parent with an agenda, and you are unable to reason with her, then the teaching very often has more to do with the parent's needs than with the child's needs. In such a case, think carefully before accepting the child.

Some parents sabotage their children. I am not referring to the parent who wants her child to stop taking lessons because of the expense, or for any other valid reason.

This is different. I am referring instead to a distressing aspect of dysfunctional parental behavior which fortunately, does not occur very often. An example of this would be a situation in which a parent decides to stop a child's lessons in spite of the youngster's progress and enthusiasm. This becomes a painful moment for both teacher and student. Again, this has to do with the parent and not with the child. An example could be the jealousy a parent feels when a child is doing well at something, and being creatively expressive. This might point up the very inadequacies a parent has or feels he has, or make him uncomfortable.

Sometimes the parent becomes jealous of the relationship the child develops with the teacher. Unable to express this, she provokes the situation by being rude or inappropriate to the teacher. In this case lessons have to be terminated.

Another difficult situation may arise if the parent is less intelligent or worldly than the child. You may speak to this parent and tell them that their son is quite talented. Say you are recommending that he study privately even though he is quite young. You say, "He is able to grasp the material. He is very flexible. He has a good sense of rhythm. He loves it."

Meanwhile, rather than spend money on a decent piano, the parent has bought a cheap electronic keyboard. You speak kindly to the parent and you say, "Ben needs a better instrument because when an instrument sounds more beautiful you want to play it more. He is at the point where he is really beginning to listen to himself. He is learning and wants to translate these notes he has learned to read onto an instrument that has more weight and authority."

The parent may respond with, "Well you see, Ben never really practices very much anyway, so I think we are just going to quit!"

This is irritating. Teacher has taken the time to give the parent wonderful feedback. She has given the parent a compliment about her son. The parent has totally missed the point, and refuses to consider the alternatives because in her mind the study of piano is about practicing and only practicing.

Her lack of intelligence comes in when she does not realize that with a better instrument this highly talented and motivated little boy will practice more. I always feel sorry for the child. The parent has a narrow world view. I have learned over the years not to argue and to just let go. There are many students in the world. To try to convince a parent otherwise is usually a waste of breath.

Here is another similar example. A very young student studies and practices for almost two years. He has a dip in his practice schedule for the first time in two years, lasting about a month. Not only is this normal, occasionally it is necessary. There is a lot of down time in the music world because one needs to think. There is a lot of thinking required at any age. We begin to learn the value of reflection as we ponder our pieces... and ourselves and the world. At any rate, you can guess the end of the story. The parent made the child quit.

Frequently threats go along with this, as in, "If you don't practice...." When the learning becomes about the child fulfilling the parent's needs, there is a good chance the endeavor will not succeed. It was perfectly all right for this child to day dream for a month or two. He was very attentive in class, absorbing all the information that came his way. Practice picks up. Just as in all our processes of life, there is a natural rhythm that each person encounters while on the path to learning.

Music students are fortunate. They are not in school, taking tests and being compared to others. When a student comes to a music studio he sits alone with his teacher and they go to work. And work is not defined as a linear structure with a series of questions to be answered after the material is presented. Work is defined as a student learning to build a bridge to this great musical presence, this musical language that is understood by all peoples everywhere. The work is about each student finding his or her voice and place in this unique universe that is varied, immense, diverse and enlightening. Why rush? The journey is magnificent.

The parent that either studied as a youth, or whose perspective of the world is insightful, the parent willing to work with the teacher, the parent who trusts the teacher, the parent who receives joy from the knowledge his child brings to him in any fashion, the parent who trusts her child, all of these traits are the qualities of the parents that most successfully support the student on her quest to become a musician.

There are some lucky parents that study music also. These lucky parents have yet another world to explore with their offspring. It is a world with it's own dimensions, language, and presence. I have one parent the other day who said to me, "Charlie was so excited to get an F# in his new scale." That's nice. Real nice. What a nice sharing.

Make-Ups

There are many ways to learn music. The experience of the piano student is a private experience. It is solo. The student frequently does not have other people with whom she might share and discuss her work. Because music is a language, it is vital that students have opportunities to interact with fellow students in order to improve their command of the language. One way to remedy this is by offering group make-ups. Another way to remedy this is to hold scheduled workshops through-out the year.

A group make-up is a one hour make-up that happens once a month for everyone between the ages of 7 and 18 that has had to miss a lesson. The make-up is open to the student that had to miss a class because of illness, or travel. The make-up is not an option for the student who chooses to miss her lesson because she has a sporting event or a birthday party to go to.

An understanding of group dynamics is essential in order to structure the make-up in a way which will be valuable for students of different ages who are grouped together on such an occasion. The first precept is that, as language binds a community together, therefore this microcosm of musical community present can speak to one another musically about their pieces. The second precept, much along Montessori lines, is that older children help younger children by their compassion, interest and the example they set. Younger children help older children by giving the older ones a chance to contribute to them and by the stimulation of memory. An older child might say, "I remember when I played that piece. Why don't you play it faster?"

A Master Class is a class where students get together and teacher takes turns teaching each one. The others learn from the experience. A lot of information is exchanged. Another advantage to the group make-up is that people get to perform in front of one another. There are many students who play quite nicely on their own, or when they are at home. It is an entirely different experience to perform in front of others, particularly your peers. The group make-up becomes an exercise in poise. Musical trouble spots that heretofore had not been present, surface and give each student a new concept of what needs to be worked on in the following weeks.

This is the structure. If the students have not met prior to the session, they should, on arrival, sit in a circle and introduce themselves.Then teacher speaks about musical principles for awhile. This can be general or more specific, depending on the age and advancement of your group. For instance, teacher might talk about musical dynamics for a bit, and ask students for examples of musical dynamics. Then the students could illustrate the musical dynamic at the keyboard after speaking about it.

Harpsichord is always a good starting point for an intriguing discussion. The history of the instrument and how modern playing is related to it makes for lively discourse. A discussion of the composers in the context of music history is also a good starting point. After some discussion, the first student plays. Although the order is not important, if a younger student is present, he can go first. Everyone claps at the end of his playing, whether he has played competently or not. It takes some nerve to get up in front of others and share your process. That is what is being acknowledged.

If there is still time after everyone has played, and teacher has made appropriate comments, then the percussion instruments can be played. There are many percussive games that are challenging to all ages and fun! (see pages 38, 66.)

All in all, at the end of the hour, everybody leaves feeling enriched. This is so valuable. The private piano lesson is not the only way to receive and transmit musical information. When we view music as a language, we are allowing ourselves to experience it in many different formats. Getting together with one's musical community, having the focus be music, talking it and playing it, is a marvelous transformation of the private and interior experience of solo piano.

It is an intelligent and efficacious way for a busy teacher to structure her time. Often constant make-ups are not possible in a successful teacher's regime. The process of group make-ups described here limits the time needed for individual make-ups and demonstrably adds to everyone's enjoyment and learning.This needs to be explained to parents. Please see Teacher Communiques in the appendix.

DISCIPLINE

When teaching a group of children it is important that they learn respect. People must learn to listen to one another without interrupting. Teacher is not to be interrupted. The instruments are not to be played when teacher is talking. There is no talking during story time.

A moment can be set aside between keyboard time and instrument time for the children to each share something with one another and with the group. Frequently kids come to class with something to say. At the appropriate time the teacher can structure this sharing moment.

Each person has "personal space". Imagine that we all have a boundary that projects from our body. What this means, particularly with rambunctious boys, is "no touching." Children are naturally warm and affectionate. I am referring to the times that boys can start kicking or shoving one another. Then we talk about respecting one another's personal space.

There is a technique for teaching people to get back into their bodies when they get wild. All children get wild at times. The Music Studio is very stimulating. It is exciting. People are encouraged to play the instruments with force. Sometimes it's great. The amount of energy generated is thrilling. Give the kids the mallets and let them bang the drums and blow off steam for a few minutes. If negative behavior persists, stop the instruments and tell them to "BREATHE!" This is an old yoga technique for "grounding energy".

"It only works if you have your feet planted firmly on the ground."

As my studio experience takes place at the keyboard and on a carpeted floor, I say, "Sit down on your butt. Put your feet flat on the floor. Take a few deep breaths. Breathe in through your nose. Exhale through your mouth. Do this three times and you will come back into touch with yourself. Your feet must be fully on the ground or it will not work. Imagine your breath traveling through your body and out your feet into the earth. Your energy will ground right into the earth."

If the children are taught this technique it works very well. Imagine. It is 4:00pm. The children coming into the studio have already had a full day at school. Let's take three first graders. Although eager to be at class they are also tired, affected by their school day, and hungry. They are finding it difficult to concentrate. Their class lasts an hour.

In the beginning of the hour they are respectful to one another and to me. As the time progresses one of the boys pushes the other in a rush to get the same instrument. Teacher calls out, "BREATHE!"

All three drop to the ground where they are. They do their "breathing". Teacher reminds them to respect one another and to respect the instruments. Teacher reminds them that there is time for everyone to play the instrument of his choice. There is no need to push. The boy that pushed is asked to apologize. Teacher also reminds them not to get into each others' personal space. "NO TOUCHING!"

When they are relaxed class resumes. This is a non-judgmental kindly exercise that can be done by anyone anywhere when the going gets rough. It can be taught to the parents for use at home and parents can use the technique as well when they feel pushed. I use it before performances to help ground my energy. All people benefit, regardless of age.

FEES

How does a piano teacher set her fees? There are a number of criteria to consider. The first is the marketplace. What is the most common rate for lessons in the area? If there is a Conservatory, call and ask the office how much the Conservatory teachers charge for a private lesson. This will generally stand for the high or expensive end of the spectrum. Then speak to your neighbors and find out what the local teachers charge for their lessons.

Depending on your qualifications and your versatility, you must make the decision on what your appropriate fee would be.

There are many factors to take into consideration. Are you a young teacher? Have you had any experience teaching? How do you feel about your musical training ? Do you like people? Can you teach piano and harpsichord? Do you know how to play guitar? Can you teach voice, run a choir, play drums?

There are many piano teachers that studied a bit when they were younger and now teach children, imparting the amount of knowledge they have accrued, to others. A teacher coming from this background would need to teach at the lower or less expensive end of the spectrum because of her lack of professional training.

If you are a teacher and composer, and can teach composition, it is appropriate to charge more. If you can teach adults as well as children it is appropriate to charge more. If you have continued your studies into adulthood and are still involved in learning music, it is appropriate to charge more. If you are a performance artist it is appropriate to charge more. If you are utilizing The Sheli Nan Method and can offer your students a variety of musical experiences along with an educated and erudite training, it is appropriate to charge on the higher end of the musical spectrum.

Of course reputations are built over time. As your students progress, your reputation will progress as well. Never be afraid to name your worth. Society tends to undervalue its music teachers. The contribution that is made to society when people are able to express themselves with creativity, depth and clarity, has no price. We are providing a vital service to those who study with us.

THE RHYTHMTWISTERS PROGRAM

AN APPLICATION OF THE SHELI NAN METHOD FOR PUBLIC AND PRIVATE SCHOOL INSTRUCTION

This program offers the student a multi-cultural and multi-ethnic introduction to music. The method emphasizes hands-on, participatory learning, primarily through the use of percussion instruments. The core aspects of musical experience and expression which the **RHYTHMTWISTERS** Program teaches, are; listening, rhythm, ensemble, dynamics, cooperation, and respect for others. The primary tools for this training are the brightly colored percussion tubes called Boomwhackers. Percussion instruments and music for those instruments provide a natural and accessible vocabulary for children, as well as adults. The instruments and rhythmic language are relevant to all musical experiences as teaching tools, expressive outlets and accompaniment.

This percussive experience is woven into all of the musical programs which the **RHYTHMTWISTERS** Program offers, providing a musical thread of continuity through which children can analyze and enjoy other forms of music, and can also appreciate other art forms. Whether students are singing, learning music theory, or participating in the musical theater program, the rhythms and musical patterns that they learn will add accompaniment, diversity and joy to the project at hand.

The first skill which the program stresses is listening because, arguably, it is the most important factor in the development of a fulfilling musical experience. When we understand how to create our own sound, listen to it, and determine an appropriate manner and moment in which to begin and end it, we are also learning how to be civilized.

RHYTHMTWISTERS will provide qualified, well trained teachers with the highest standards of conduct and musical education to instruct children of all ages. Each teacher will be trained and supervised to assure the quality and integrity of the program instruction.

RHYTHMTWISTERS will provide an optional after school program designed to meet the needs of the school's population. The after school program will be structured as a sign-up program for interested students. A minimum number of students are required in order for the programs to be viable. At the school's request, **RHYTHMTWISTERS** will design and purchase a more extensive library of musical instruments to meet the specific needs of the school's students.

These are the programs and services that RHYTHMTWISTERS offers:

THE BASIC PERCUSSION PACKAGE: This program, which provides the essential training, is offered to all age groups. Beginning with the Boomwhacker instruments, children learn how to communicate by using musical language. As the children learn the patterns and become more comfortable listening for relevant beats, the children gradually progress to more complex patterns. The kids are encouraged to use their bodies when they play. Each week new beats and patterns are added. Subsequently, choreography and voices are also incorporated. The final stage includes opportunities for students to perform solos. If a school assembly, such as Winter Concert, is on the calendar, the students will perform in it. That event will then feature a coordinated group of musicians focusing on a presentation that allows each person to "speak" the musical language and create a unique, joyous sound!

CHOIR: Besides the traditional vocal training that includes posture, projection, the placement of teeth, tongue and lips, and the basic concepts of solfeggio, the **RHYTHMTWISTERS** Choir teaches the Nigerian method of Call and Response. Students also use the Boomwhackers as a training tool in this choir program. These percussion instruments provide a stimulating counterpoint to the singing and help to clarify aspects of timing and the counting of beats. The element of timing is clarified by the percussion. As the children learn songs from many cultures they are also learning how to accompany themselves with the Boomwhackers.

DRUM CIRCLE: This class is especially appropriate for the older children and does require instruments. (more info on instruments in the next chapter) Within the RHYTHMTWISTERS Drum Circle the emphasis is on cooperation, the joy of large sounds, and the ability to listen carefully and learn profoundly. Drum Circle requires a commitment to community. Our teachers are trained in the art of creating community and in this class the children quickly realize that in order to make music successfully, they need to think carefully, be respectful of others, and coordinate their movements with each other. The training is derived from Nigerian Master Drummer Babatunde Olatunji.

MUSICAL THEATER: This long term class explores the creation of a musical theater work. Staging, scenery, lighting, content, music, and drama are some of the elements which the class will discuss. Depending on the age of the participants, students and teacher will either create a scene of their own, or will develop one from an extant musical. In either case the teacher will provide appropriate guidance. The material for the piece will draw on aspects of various cultures and a scene will then take shape that can be performed for a school assembly.

PIANO & GUITAR & DRUM & VOICE CLINICS: After school private lessons, classes and clinics will be offered for children who are interested in further pursing their musical studies. The folk guitar clinics will contain up to six people each, and the African drum clinics will be structured to accommodate up to 12 people. The classical piano and voice clinics will contain up to three students each. The private lessons will be one on one. Percussion will be explored in each of these areas.

MUSIC THEORY: This course is intended for the more serious minded student who would really like to learn the mechanics of music. For students who are already playing an instrument outside of school this would be an excellent forum for studying composition. For those who are just beginning to explore music, this class would be an excellent introduction to the art form. The children will learn to read music and will have the opportunity to enhance their ability to understand the dynamics of the musical language. Some aspects of music history will also be included as well as a discussion of the importance of harpsichord. The use of Boomwhackers to illustrate rhythmic themes will enhance the learning process.

TEACHER CONCERTS: RHYTHMTWISTERS will present a teacher's concert during the spring term on a date to be determined by the school. The concert will be a benefit for the school's music program. One third of all money collected from ticket sales will be donated to the school by **RHYTHMTWISTERS** to be used for the enhancement of the school's music program.

EQUIPMENT AND MATERIAL COSTS: The School will be obligated to buy an agreed upon number of Boomwhackers. These inexpensive instruments will then become the property of the school. They can be used in all of the different formats described above. For the drum circle there are a variety of inexpensive ways to procure instruments. For the guitar clinics, children will need to provide their own instruments. A piano will be necessary for the piano classes and lessons and it would be helpful to have access to one for the choir although it is not absolutely necessary as our teachers also play guitar. The school instruments can be used for the drum clinics or private lessons. The music theory class will require a small materials charge for music paper and other necessary materials.

The **RHYTHMTWISTERS** Program can also benefit the school through various curriculum tie-ins. These could include the following topics:

Art: Students can depict the instruments.

Geography: The children can listen to recordings of African and Western music. (A hand-out with teacher suggestions is available to all who inquire.)

Thinking & Focus Skills: As mentioned above, the instruments and the activities involved in the **RHYTHMTWISTERS** Program require children to listen carefully - to themselves, one another, and the teacher. Development of this skill is obviously desirable for all scholastic subjects and activities.

Math: Rhythmic training, counting, and understanding of the sub-division of beats, are important elements in understanding mathematics. Most recent findings show that a study of music greatly enhances a person's ability to reason mathematically.

Physical Coordination/Dancing: Our sense of natural rhythm evolves from our bodies. When music is taught with a physical component it is enjoyable, invigorating, and easier to understand. Our body movements coordinated with the rhythmic training enhance our ability to count.

Conceptual Thinking: Students who learn how to understand their respective roles and places in a musical design, by anticipating appropriate points at which to play their parts, are also learning how to think conceptually. The children learn to communicate their skills with one another experiencing the joy of original creativity. This joy of learning translates into all other activities. Each person learns in an internal and external way to be communicative and responsible musically. The amount of focus necessary to accomplish these tasks will teach the children to follow through in all their endeavors.

Hands-On Classroom Application Of The Rhythmtwisters Program

When a **RHYTHMTWISTERS** Program teacher enters a fourth grade class for the first time, she begins by introducing herself and the instruments. She then asks the children to form a circle and sit on the floor. After everyone has introduced themselves, it is fun to engage in some banter with the kids, such as: "Well you know, I'll never remember all of your names today, but I am sure over the coming weeks I'll get better at it. Who remembers my name?"

Always take time to get to know your group and to gauge the general mood. It helps to spend a few moments with the main teacher beforehand in order to get a reading on how she runs her class. She may also tell you which kids to watch out for. Even troublemakers have a place in this program. It is important to understand how to create a dynamic where, instead of disrupting the proceeding, these children become empowered in a positive manner and actually help you. After some banter with the kids, hand out the percussion tubes, or ask two "helpers" to hand out these instruments, two to each child. (Remember that part of the agreement is that the school buy these extremely inexpensive instruments. Make sure you have tallied the amount correctly so that each child in the largest class you teach can hold two Boomwhackers.)

Immediate chaos will result. It is exciting to hold these instruments of different colors and sizes.Reassure them that they are going to be able to play with the tubes many times and will get to switch them as times goes on. After the children have had a chance to initially experiment with the instruments, tell them: "We are always going to have free time where you can make your own patterns up. Now let me show you exactly how to play these so that they don't break."

Then take a moment to explain that the instruments should be struck together toward the top of each Boomwhacker. Then explain that they can also be used on your body: "Try using your head for once!"

They can also be struck against the floor. It is not a good idea to strike a desk or chair, however, because the tubes can easily rupture and then you are out an instrument. Wear and tear will result no matter what, but the instrument's life can be lengthened if the children take basic precautions with them.

"Now let me ask all of you, what can you absolutely NOT DO with these instruments? Correct. Hit anyone else! These instruments are for you to use only in your personal space. I am a very mellow teacher and you are going to have a lot of fun, but you are going to understand right off the bat that we must have respect for these instruments and for one another and in no way do I want to see anyone hitting anyone else with them!"

That clarifies the limits with the instruments. Now we start with the basics.

"Everyone in this room can count to four. Let's go. Play your tubes and keep the count of four. BUT keep the count in your head. Do not say it aloud."

At this point you begin to lead the kids hitting the tubes straight in a count of four. Once you have established this beat and everyone is playing together, tell the kids that you are now going to alter the beat and that they have to follow. There should be no talking at this point. Alter the beat by dropping the fourth beat so that your count is 1-2-3-rest-and continue like this for awhile. Some kids will get this very quickly. Others won't. After this is comfortable, once again, warn the kids and tell them you are going to change the beat again. This time, do 1-2-rest-rest-. After this go to 1-rest-rest-4-1-rest-rest-4-, then 1-rest-3-rest-then rest-2-rest-4 etc. There are many variations on the four beats as mentioned. Do as many as the group can sustain for the first class, perhaps in the ten minute range. As the children get more sophisticated, you may stop in the middle of a pattern and ask, "Where are we in the beat? Can anyone tell me?"

Usually there will be someone who can say, "We are on 2." This usually signifies the beginning of listening. This is the warm-up.

The next exercise begins like this. Ask the child on your right to make up an easy pattern, anything the student likes. Once that student has created this pattern, he or she must repeat it four times. Then the group joins in and plays it four times with the student. You might want to start by giving an example that you make up, perhaps something like this. Hit the floor once with your tubes, clap them twice, and then hit the floor once more. That would serve as a pattern. Then you would repeat that four times. Then the class would join in and do it with you. Then go around in the circle and give each child a chance to do the same. Watch to see if your group can accurately copy the pattern that is being made up. Continue until all of the children have had a turn.

Discipline will be a factor. Some kids either can't sit still, or talk all of the time. At the beginning, remember their names as best you can because it is very effective for a new teacher to say, "George, come sit right next to me. You are going to be my helper today." This is one technique—slight embarrassment along with getting to sit next to teacher. That way the teacher can keep an eye on the child and he knows it! Do not hesitate to change student's places if they talk too much. Separate two boys and put a girl in between. Make kids change seats from across the circle. Discipline issues hopefully won't go on for long because the Boomwhackers are exciting and the students respond very well to this training. They really enjoy it. It is a pleasure to use their bodies after being cooped up at desks for hours, and the sounds are empowering and fascinating.

The next exercise is called "Conversations". Ask kids what a conversation is. Have a conversation about conversations. "What is a conversation exactly? Do people have the same kinds of conversations? When you are out on the field or hard top is everyone speaking to each other in the same way? What are some of the differences and what are some of the similarities?" The children can either raise their hands or you can have a conversation with them if they are responding in a way that you feel is appropriate.

"Okay. So we can have happy conversations and angry conversations. We can talk about new toys with our friends and we can be pretty excited about things. And then there are other times when we just shrug our shoulders and don't really talk about anything. There are so many ways to communicate with one another. I want two volunteers now to come into the circle and have a conversation with one another. Please do this standing up. I want the rest of you to figure out what their conversation is about. There is one rule, though. NO TALKING. How are they going to have a conversation without talking? They are going to use their Boomwhackers. Let's listen carefully and see if we can get the idea. Are they communicating something happy? Something sad? Are they angry with one another?"

This is a theme that can be endlessly varied by the teacher. Although the kids will understand the moods of their fellow students easily, when the class has been running for a few weeks, the conversations between the students taking part in this exercise will have developed rhythms of their own. For instance,

"Today, when you speak to one another, let's take a look at the beginning, the middle and the end of your conversation. Perhaps, if you are angry at one another, you can start off quietly. Then one person can "say" something to the other person that irritates him. Then the Boomwhackers can get louder. All of a sudden you are having a fight. Then one of you will realize that it's a drag to fight and will have to apologize, or at least say, hey, let's not do this anymore. Then the other person will have to agree, and you will just make up. What we want today is a conversation that has all three elements that I have just discussed. A beginning, a middle and an end."

The children are fascinated by exercises like these. They improve their communication skills. They learn how to listen to their fellow students. They become more physically coordinated. They relate to one another musically learning the basics of respect. Rhythm becomes a means of self expression. They are also using music as a means of conveying emotions and events.

You are now getting to the end of your 45 minute class. Ask two children to gather up the Boomwhackers and tell your class that you ALWAYS expect them to thank you at the end of the period.

"Thank you Sheli for teaching us."

The 45 minutes that have gone by are delightful. Frequently the kids will come up and hug you afterwards. This is the program in a nutshell. It continues to expand in profundity because each of these exercises can become more complex as the class becomes more savvy. Once the students have mastered the above material, they can attempt more advanced exercises. Remember, however, that you are meeting with them once a week. It takes times to learn the basics.

Here is an example of a more complex exercise. The children break into groups of four. Two children sit facing one another and two children stand facing one another to the sides of the children that are sitting so that a 3 dimensional square is formed. The children clap their Boomwhackers twice and then one child in each pair strikes the other child's Boomwhackers twice. This is a pattern that has four components. This pattern repeats four or eight times and then the person who is striking the other person's Boomwhackers becomes the one who's tubes are struck. All four kids do this at once, both those that are standing and those that are sitting. This takes coordination and concentration. Clap clap, hit hit, clap clap, hit hit etc. and then clap clap hit hit - but now the kids who were hitting tubes are now holding out their tubes for the other children to strike. The switch occurs after the pattern has been repeated four or eight times. The process needs to be quick and all four kids have to be in sync.

Creative teachers who have studied percussion will be able to create their own exercises as time goes on. This is encouraged.

The basics of this program are incorporated into all of the other programs listed above. The Boomwhackers are very effective for the RHYTHMTWISTERS choir, as they provide another musical element and teach the children the basics of rhythm. For example, perhaps you'll be singing "Michael Row the Boat Ashore" with your students. It is possible to incorporate a rhythmic pattern with the Boomwhackers so that the children are singing and playing. I chose this particular example because, in a class I taught, the children decided it would be fun to "row" with their percussion tubes also! Instead of saying no, I went along with it and it was really quite charming. The kids stood and sang, playing the beat with their instruments the first time. The second time they got on the floor and sang while using the Boomwhackers, somewhat in time, to "row". Children come up with wonderful variations themselves. It is important to be open to what they have to offer. The RHYTHMTWISTERS Program has time for creativity and new ideas. Our philosophy is that much is learned in many different directions. We can learn from teacher, from student, from one another, from the instruments, etc.

Another significant aspect of the RHYTHMTWISTERS Program is the way it brings students into focus. It is a healthy, creative, and constructive way for children to channel and release pent-up energy. The main teachers are usually pleased because, after a RHYTHMTWISTERS Program class, their students are often more motivated and better behaved.

The RHYTHMTWISTERS drum circle, for older children, is a challenge of a different sort. If you are working with preadolescents and adolescents, from grades 6-8, other needs must be addressed. For one thing, the Boomwhackers are not big enough or loud enough to satisfy this age group. Because many schools are strapped for cash, it is possible for the school to buy plastic buckets, two per child, and drum sticks. If it is possible, ask the school to buy two sets of drumsticks per child enrolled in this class so that the kids can take a pair home to practice. This is an inexpensive way to provide basic rhythmic musical training for the children.

Because a teacher who is not experienced with this age group might find this class rather challenging, I would suggest giving careful thought to structuring the process. Limit the class size to 12 students.

In the beginning these children may be resentful, somewhat hostile and curious. Frequently the kids are big. And loud. Do not give out the sticks immediately. Begin the class like this.

"My name is Sheli and I am here to teach you how to drum. We are going to learn patterns that come from an ancient African tradition. Babatunde Olatunji is a great Master Drummer from Nigeria. He came to this country as a young man. He was chosen to come here in the 1950s to study engineering. He brought the African Yoruba drumming tradition to the United States and he created a language for us on the drums so that we could learn how to play the drums and make the drums speak to one another. Before I teach this to you I am going to lay out for you what I expect and I want you to listen very carefully. Musicians must create a sense of community in order to be able to play with one another successfully. What does this mean exactly? It means that if any of you are angry with one another, you leave the fight at the door before you come in. This is a place where we will learn to create together and there is to be no putting anyone down or making fun of anyone else. Do you understand? This is my first rule. EVERYONE gets a chance here. There is room for everyone. What is drumming? Commitment to community. What are we doing here? Creating a community. Every week when you come in I am going to ask you what are we doing here? You are going to answer me by saying, "Music is commitment to community." Say it now. Remember that."

This point will need to be reiterated every time you see your kids. This is a more distracted and difficult age group. I call them the hormonally challenged! Often, right at the beginning, some kids will misbehave, or not listen. I have developed a wonderful strategy for these kids. It is always the greatest desire of the **RHYTHMTWISTERS** Program to include everyone in this quest for musical competence. We never want to kick anyone out of class. That is truly the very last measure to take. Therefore, I have developed a new strategy for dealing with hyperactive kids. Take a corner of the room and make it the dancing corner.

"We are always going to meet in circle. If you arrive in the room before I do I want to see your chairs set up and I want each of you to have two drums (buckets) in front of you. Behind the circle, near the blackboard we are going to have the dance space. Listen carefully. I know that it is hard for some of you to sit still. You might feel like you would really like to talk, fuss with your neighbor, or disrupt the class. I don't want to kick you out. Therefore, the dancing corner will be your spot. If you just feel like you are having an energy rush and really need to work it off, GO DANCE. Now let me clarify this for you. The dancers are not permitted to TOUCH one another.

These are the same rules as in the circle. NO TOUCHING!!! And the dancers are not permitted to speak to one another. You just go dance and work off some energy and then come back and quietly resume your seat so that you do not distract the circle. There will be plenty of music for you to dance to."

It is quite extraordinary to watch the kids because they do take advantage of this. Particularly the boys. Frequently there are many great dancers. When kids do get up to do their dancing, others will jeer. Shut them up immediately and complement the dancers.

"You dance so beautifully. I love watching you."

In classes such as these the group dynamics are as important as the music you are teaching. It is essential to address what happens socially between the children in order for the children to surrender those parts of themselves that will allow them to express themselves musically.

The class begins with five minutes of free time. This is heartily recommended because the kids have so much energy. Ask the school to place the class in a classroom away from the main part of the school because a lot of noise will be made. Hand out the sticks to your kids with the admonishments,

"What are the rules? Right. No touching. No hitting anyone else. Watch out with your sticks."

Almost the worst thing that can happen to a child in this class is to have his sticks taken away. Do not hesitate to do this if they are being disruptive, talking way too much, etc. Tell them they will get their sticks back in 5 minutes if they behave. Remind them to go dance if they can't sit still.

After five minutes of warm-up, begin by teaching the Olatunji exercises. With the sticks, begin with the right hand. Allow the stick to fall in the middle of the drum head. Tell the students that the name of this sound is "GN". Have them do this a number of times with the right hand. After that take the stick and let it fall towards the rim of the drum head on the right side towards the student's body. Tell them this is "GO" then have them take the stick with the left hand and hit once again on the rim of the drum head this time on the left side close to the student's body. This is "DO". The entire pattern is GN GO DO. The right hand hits in the middle of the drum head for GN, drops down to the right hand rim side for GO and the left hand hits on the left hand rim side DO. That's it for the first lesson. It will be hard for a number of kids to make the right hand do the first two beats. As the children progress please use the percussion chart on page 91.

The second exercise is the same as the one that was done in the fourth grade class. People are encouraged to make up their own beats, repeat them four times, and then have the group join in. Be the first example. Make up an easy pattern, such as, right hand stick hit once, left hand stick hit once, right hand stick hit twice, left hand stick hit once. Show the kids the pattern. Repeat it four times and have them join in. Go slow. After they get the hang of it, go around in the circle. Have each kid make up a pattern. Complement each kid. The pattern can be easy. This is perfectly okay. Be encouraging. Do not allow anyone to tease anyone else. Remind people that no pattern belongs to anyone and that anyone can do a pattern that is somewhat like someone else's and it is perfectly okay. Remember at all times to have as much fun as possible. Always be on the look out for talent. If someone comes up with a really great pattern, build on it. Take a moment to incorporate a simple counterpoint by another child to the original pattern. For instance, one kid can beat a straight four with his stick on the leg of his chair, while the other kid does his own pattern. Once the class gets going, you can have kids add different "voices" to patterns that lend themselves to building musical conversations. At the beginning though, each child gets a chance to create his or her own individual pattern.

Once that has taken place, stop and talk with the kids for awhile. Tell them how well they have done. Ask them what they like to do out of school. Just relax for a moment. Then do the conversation exercises that were described for the fourth grade class. Follow the same pattern as outlined previously.

I have had many incredible experiences teaching this class. Once, two kids decided to have a musical argument with one another. This class had already been in session for a number of weeks so the children knew the rules and what was expected of them. It got so exciting that the rest of us just joined in. (Including me!) We couldn't help ourselves. When the playing quieted down, I exclaimed, "You know what just happened? We had a rumble. But what was the difference?" One of the kids said, "Nobody got hurt!!!"

It was so exciting. We were cooking in that class. I said, "How can we end it really well?" The same kid came up with a pattern on the drum. "I'm sorry, I'm sorry..."

This was played right left left, right left left. It was a breakthrough moment. We all played that pattern and left the class feeling very satisfied (Especially me!). The trick is to know when to let go and when to discipline. This comes with time. For all teachers beginning to teach this way, have patience. You will make many mistakes. Courage love and perseverance will teach you how to overcome the obstacles that these children face on a daily basis in their lives. If we can somehow give them another choice in the ways they communicate with each other, and if we can give them another way to process their own private thoughts, we have contributed toward creating a more peaceful universe.

APPENDIX

I have organized this material to assist you in the setup and the smooth management of your studio.

Firstly I have given you two separate examples of the Bach Minuet in G Major from the Anna Magdalena Bach Notebook. This example is from the Baerenreiter Urtext Edition; Leichte Klavierstucke und Tanze. The first example has been notated with a slash to remind the student where to separate the voices (articulation). The second example uses our current notation to enhance a baroque interpretation of the piece. Each example of notation has the same meaning. In this second example, a staccato is not a staccato. It is an indication of an articulated note. A slur is not a phrase. It indicates super legato.

The next section of the Appendix presents Teacher Communiques. I have included a contract entitled Music Studio Guidelines. This contract contains a payment schedule. After this, there is a Baroque note from The Music Studio. Continuing on, there is also a Fall Welcome note, Spring and Summer Greetings and a RHYTHMTWISTERS note. When I host a Student Gathering I also address the parents before the event. On the last page of Teacher Communiques I have sketched out some ideas for your use.

The third section contains Sample Pages from Students' Notebooks. Once again these are taken from actual notes that I have written up for my students after each lesson.

In the fourth section there is an introduction to Nigerian Master Drummer Babatunde Olatunji and there is a chart of his percussion patterns.

After this there are some actual Group Lesson Plans that I wrote for a teacher that was substituting for me.

I thought it would be fun to include some photos of students who have studied with me throughout the years. Hence, the Student Photo Gallery.

There is a page of Story Ideas and then the Instrument List with Illustrations.

I have written out the Scale and Arpeggio Charts and I include a diagram of the Circle of Fifths.

The last three sections begin with Recommended Editions, go on to the Glossary, and end with the Bibliography.

For information on how to order books or cds please see the last page of the book.

1. Menuet G-dur

BWV Anh. 114

Christian Petzold
(1677-1733)

1. Menuet G-dur

BWV Anh. 114

Christian Petzold
(1677-1733)

BA 6572

MUSIC STUDIO GUIDELINES

PLEASE read the following carefully since it forms the basis of our mutual understanding regarding lesson-taking. I'll be happy to discuss any aspect of this policy with you. I am pleased to welcome my new assistant to The Music Studio this year. She will have her own roster of students and she will teach for me throughout the school year for approximately 14 scattered days, and I will occasionally teach for her. She will also be teaching the group children's program, **RHYTHMTWISTERS**, and TUNETWISTERS, that I originated, here and at The Piedmont Piano Music School.

CALENDAR

Lessons begin	September 4
Thanksgiving Holidays	November 27-29
Winter Break	December 23 - January 3
Martin Luther King Day	January 19
President's Day	February 16
Spring Break	April 11-17
Memorial Day	May 25
Summer Schedule begins	June 29

TUITION

Tuition is based on 39 private lessons and 1 vacation day during the academic year, September 4th through June 27th. Tuition includes teacher consultation, preparation time for lessons, workshops, Junior Bach Festival prep and recitals. Fees are averaged for the academic year to make ten equal payments. Summer lessons are separate and are prorated. Payment is due by the first lesson of the month.

MAKE-UPS

MAKE-UPS are limited to one time per month. (The exception in this case is for illness. If someone is ill for more than one week, please talk to me so that we can adjust the schedule accordingly.) The fourth Thursday of every month, from 5-6pm, I will host a group make-up. This will run along the lines of a children's Master Class. It will be an informative, lively and enjoyable way for the children to share their work with one another. Make-ups will be given for illness and travel. They will not be given for birthday parties, sports or other activities.

PAYMENT SCHEDULE

Monthly tuition is:	______	for 30 minute lessons
	______	for 45 minute lessons
	______	for 1-hour lessons
TuneTwisters	______	for 30 minute shared lessons (2 children)
RhythmTwisters	______	for 30 minute group lessons (3 children)
Semester payment	______	for 30 minute lessons
September - December	______	for 45 minute lessons
	______	for 1-hour lessons
	______	for 30 minute shared lessons (2 children)
	______	for 30 minute group lessons (3 children)
January-March &	______	for 30 minute lessons
April-June	______	for 45 minute lessons
	______	for 1-hour lessons
	______	for 30 minute shared lessons (2 children)
	______	for 30 minute group lessons (3 children)

Thank you so much. It is my pleasure to serve as intelligent and creative a community as all of you represent.

You/your child is scheduled for DAY: ________
TIME: ________

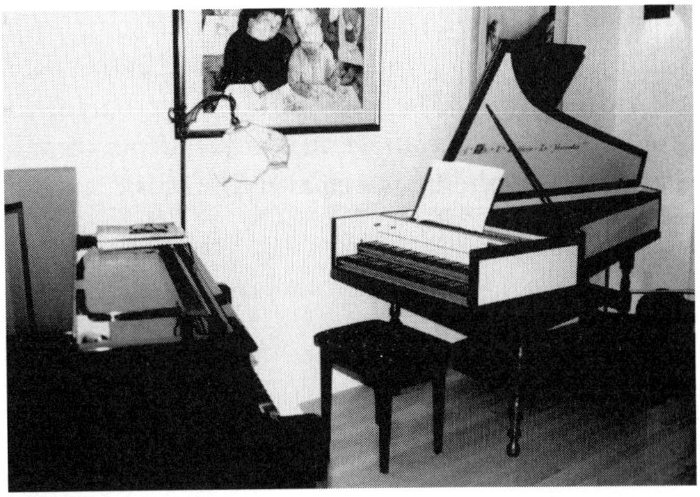

A Baroque Note From The Music Studio

I would like to start a new program this year at The Music Studio. As you all know, all of my students play harpsichord. This has become one of the hallmarks of advanced learning. When a student reaches a certaincompetency, he then begins to play the Baroque music on the instrument it was composed for. This is an exciting and unique moment in the life of the keyboard player.

What I would like to do this year is begin some of the children on the harpsichord at a younger age. The commitment it would require is that the families interested buy a harpsichord. Harpsichords come in different prices starting at about $2000.00 and going up steeply to $16,000.00 or more for a professional instrument.

The student who owns a harpsichord can begin the study with me concurrent with her piano studies, at a much younger age. I am thinking about even starting the little ones. I have a very exciting repertoire to teach. For example, I will teach from the book Leopold Mozart composed to teach little Wolfgang on. Wolfgang Amadeus Mozart had a harpsichord at his home and began his keyboard studies there. Many of the pieces of his youth were written for that very instrument. I will also teach the Bach family and the many composers from that era.

Music is a lifetime endeavor. It outlasts sports, dance and many of the activities we do as youth. Playing harpsichord is a mark of distinction and quality education. As the history of keyboard music is only about 500 years old, and harpsichord occupied center stage for 200 of those years, (1590-1790), there is an amazing amount to learn about the development of music from this instrument, the composers who composed for this instrument, not to mention the joy and complexity the instrument challenges us with. We would be the only studio in the Bay Area, and perhaps one of the few in the world, where smaller children would learn harpsichord.

Aside from the cost of the instrument itself there would no extra charge in the teaching. This year for the first time there will be an Early Music Society chapter for younger keyboard players. There will also be auditions for the Junior Bach Festival. I frequently hold harpsichord workshops with my students and harpsichord master classes with visiting colleagues. This is a fascinating community to join and children and parents alike would profit greatly by the intellect and talent that comprise it.

Please call me if you would be interested in this program. I am very excited by the prospect of it and would encourage all of my students, regardless of age, to buy a harpsichord for practice at home as well as at The Music Studio.

Let me know.

Love,

Sheli

Fall Welcome Note From The Music Studio

Dear Parents and Students,

Welcome back to The Music Studio. Thus another year begins and we are settling in for a wonderful season. It is amazing to see so many people return who have grown both physically and intellectually from stimulating experiences over the summer. We will apply that new found knowledge and enthusiasm to our musical studies this year. We will have meaningful results.

Remember that as we return to more demanding schedules it will take awhile for some of the children to come back into focus. Practice and the expectations that teacher has for her students will reassert itself as the modus operandi. Patience please. Do not push. Give the process a chance to unfold. We have our whole lives to study music, thankfully. We are not on a time line. There are many ways to learn. Trust your kids and trust yourselves.

There are a few announcements. The first is that for those of you who have expressed interest in the harpsichord program, this week I will have three harpsichords in my studio for you to view. They are in the $3000.00 category. They are probably somewhat negotiable. Please come in when your child has a lesson and check them out or give me a call. I would be delighted to show them to you. If you are an adult student, please consider one for yourself.

As mentioned before, this will be one of the few programs worldwide where smaller people are taught harpsichord along with piano from a young age. It is a thrilling opportunity for the family interested in this degree of scholarship.

The make-up schedule for the next four months will be Thursday:

September 25th	5:30-6:30
October 30th	same
November 20th	same
December 18th	same

Let's have a great year!!!

Love,

Sheli

SPRING GREETINGS FROM THE MUSIC STUDIO

HI EVERYONE! It's good to be back. I trust you all had a lovely and instructive time with my assistant. We were indeed lucky to have her as she had just finished a teaching stint at the Conservatory of San Francisco.

Well, now it is time to gear up for the Student Gathering and the coming summer. I would like to go over a few changes in The Music Studio with all of you. But before this, I would like to announce with pleasure that our very talented student, age 13, was accepted into the Junior Bach Festival this year and performed on harpsichord. This is a very difficult competition that chooses only the most advanced students in the Bay Area. Congratulations to her and her family. We look forward to hearing her perform at the Student Gathering.

For the summer months I will be available to teach you or your child. It is a wonderful time to study because there is no homework, and many less distractions. My schedule is wide open so that you can fashion an agenda that fits your plans. For instance, you can take one lesson, or two or skip some weeks etc. For the students in group classes you might want to consider some private lessons over the summer. It would also be fine to continue the group classes if we choose a day and date for all concerned. One Mom could call me and we could set up a summer program. We could be very flexible so that everyone would get what they need.

For the Fall I am making some changes in the way I run the Studio. I will have an assistant that will begin teaching the group classes (with the exception of the Saturday morning classes). My assistant, personally trained by me in my method, will also teach some private lessons. At present the group classes will run through second grade. By the end of second grade children will be eligible for private lessons or semiprivate lessons. This means that after second grade a child will either take privately, or with one other child for half an hour. This arrangement will allow the children to learn to read and play music. It keeps the price down and is an enjoyable way for two people who are friends to share a learning experience. This shared class is most beneficial when the student takes a private lesson once a month or so. Then the learning in group is reinforced and reading can be stressed.

Everyone enjoys some private time as well. Although my assistant is taking over some of my student load, I will be supervising and checking in on the lessons monthly. My assistant will be teaching my method, under my tutelage at The Music Studio. So for those children that I am recommending continuing to study with my assistant, I will still be a presence and will oversee all that goes on here. I will be taking less students. This coming year I am going to finish my book, (I wrote 60 pages on my vacation) and I am eager to continue composing. I have written in a recommendation for you/or your child at the end of this note that I hope will work for you. Please let me know immediately as I already have a waiting list for the summer and well into next year.

I am currently training three teachers in my method. One of the teachers will work for me. Others will be using the method in their own studios, as well as at The

Piedmont Music School. I have a great deal of confidence in the people I am training and therefore I can offer to you the same quality of teacher ability, intelligence, thoughtfulness and creativity that is the hallmark of this Studio. Piedmont Piano is also offering my method, with teachers trained by me, beginning in September. I look forward to hearing from you all at the soonest possible time and with that I wish you a wonderful spring and look forward to our Student Gathering.

Sincerely,

Sheli

My recommendation for __________ is __________ on ________ .
This new schedule begins in the fall.

THE MONDAY GROUP FROM 4:00-5:00PM. THE STUDENT GATHERING IS MONDAY JUNE 9th AT 4:30. PARENTS INVITED.

THE TUESDAY GROUP FROM 3:00-3:30. THE STUDENT GATHERING IS TUESDAY MAY 27th AT 3:10. PARENTS INVITED.

THE WEDNESDAY GROUP FROM 4:00-5:00PM.THE STUDENT GATHERING IS WEDNESDAY MAY 28th 4:30. PARENTS INVITED.

THE SATURDAY GROUP FROM 9:00-9:30AM. THE STUDENT GATHERING IS SATURDAY JUNE 14th AT 9:10. PARENTS INVITED.

THE ADVANCED STUDENT GATHERING IS SUNDAY NIGHT JUNE 8th AT 7:00PM.

THE STUDENT GATHERING FOR EVERYONE ELSE IS ON SUNDAY JUNE 15th AT 3:00PM.

A short reminder - private lessons are a 10 month commitment and run through the end of June. If your child is leaving town early, please be sure to contact me so that he/she can receive all of her lessons beforehand.

Thanks.

Summer Greetings From The Music Studio

Dear Students Parents and Friends of THE MUSIC STUDIO:

Greetings to all of you. Please take a few moments to review the enclosed material. I am reorganizing THE MUSIC STUDIO for the coming year in order to best meet the needs of our musical community. This summer I will be codifying THE SHELI NAN METHOD. This method is unique because it offers a wide range of musical experience to all of the students. There are many important facets of musical expression that are taught and experienced in my lessons. The first is the study of classical piano. This is based on my own classical training, handed down to me by my most excellent teachers throughout the years. The second is my familiarity and my training with Ethnic Music, most notably the music of Cuba and Africa. This music is taught both at the keyboard, guitar, voice, and on the percussion instruments. The third facet of my method is that of composition. This is an integral part of my training, teaching people how to express themselves.

I am going to be adding an exciting new option to The Music Studio curriculum. I will be teaching groups of 3 children a more advanced serious piano course. This class will cost _____ a month, plus book fees, whether there are four or five classes monthly. It will run for one hour. This is the logical next step for the children graduating from the pre-piano RHYTHMTWISTERS classes. Children can stay with their original groups or move to different groups. It also serves the older children who are more advanced. The advantage of structuring the class this way is that the children will get more time with me. They will be able to learn in an environment that is supportive of them and they will continue to be supportive of their peers. The sharing of information and the learning process will be enhanced by the group experience. We will all be on piano. We will study piano together and we will also spend a short part of our hour continuing our percussion training. This class will be less expensive than private lessons are and will offer the option of continued percussion and composition. The philosophy of THE MUSIC STUDIO is all inclusive. Students here have access to everything from the Baroque period, re: harpsichord, to Afro-Cuban rhythms re: conga and percussion instruments.

I also will be offering the very same set-up for my guitar students. These classes will teach folk guitar and percussion. Often learning in group is an enjoyable way to absorb the musical language. I will have 3 guitars in the studio so that students coming directly from school can choose to use one of my guitars or to bring their own. Once again the classes will run for one hour and cost______monthly.

The third class that I am offering is for the Adult students. Many of you have expressed an interest in performance outside of our usual GALA Student Gathering which takes place every four months. I will be offering Master Classes for those ofyou interested in working on your pieces "in process" with others. The classes will be limited to 3 students although if more of you sign up, we will extend the class time to accommodate everyone. You are also invited to sit in without talking part if you would like to listen to the teaching. This is a marvelous way to learn. You will learn about the different composers by listening to the feedback I give others, and you will have a chance to share your own growth and understanding of your piece. You can choose something outside of your normal class schedule that we can work on only in Master Class, or you can play one of your current pieces. We can also decide as a group if we would like to tackle, for instance, the Russian composers for a series of Master Classes, etc. The Master Class will meet on the fourth Thursday of every month at 8:00 pm. The price will be _____ per person for 2, _____ per person for three or more. The class will generally run for more than an hour.

For the coming year "Make-ups" will be limited to one time per month. (The exception in this case is for illness. If someone is ill for more than one week, please talk to me so that we can adjust the schedule accordingly.) The fourth Thursday of every month, from 5:00pm-6:00pm, I will host a group make-up. This will run along the lines of a children's Master Class. It will be an informative, lively and enjoyable way for the children to share their work with one another.

There is a new fee schedule for the coming year. I have also included a weekly calendar and I have penciled in a place where I think your child could participate. Please check this and let me now as soon as possible if this works for you because space is limited.

In September I will be hiring and training an assistant. Sam and I have been invited on a trip to Africa in mid March. By March, I will have all of the scheduling in place so that my assistant can teach in the interim when I am gone. It is important to maintain our schedules.

For the coming year the weeks that I will take off as vacation time will be correlated as closely as possible to the school calendar for winter and spring vacations. These vacation times will in effect be a trade for the extra lessons that are taught at no charge through-out the year, when there are five rather than four weeks per month. These vacation days are not to be confused with paid holidays such as Labor Day or Memorial Day. In September I will be sending out our yearly calendar of holidays and vacation times.

For the summer time I will be available for any classes or lessons that you desire. Summer is much less scheduled at The Music Studio and everyone that studies with me over the summer is guaranteed a place in the fall.

Thank you so much. It is my pleasure to serve as intelligent and creative a community as all of you represent.

Sincerely,

Sheli Nan

RHYTHMTWISTERS NOTES FROM THE MUSIC STUDIO

THE MUSIC STUDIO is pleased to announce classes beginning in September for pre-pre-piano and pre-piano, RHYTHMTWISTERS, and TUNETWISTERS. These classes are limited to three children each and run for half an hour on Saturday mornings. The ages are 3 years old to 5 years old. This is an ideal program for children interested in music and is an excellent precursor to private piano, guitar or voice lessons. Many of my current students are alumni of this effective program. The classes will run from 9:00-9:30, 9:30-10:00, and 10:00-10:30. The cost is _____ per class.

What do we do in the half-hour that we are together? We first sit at the piano and I tell a story. The children illustrate the story musically. For instance, I tell a story that has a storm in it. The children then begin to play the "storm". After story time, we learn rudimentary finger exercises at the piano. It is not necessary to have a piano or keyboard at home at this time, although it is always a wonderful idea to have a keyboard of some sort. After this, each child gets to "make something up" by him/herself at the keyboard while we all listen. Many of my alumni students are composers. I believe in teaching improvisation at the very beginning as a way of each child making the musical experience truly his or her own. When we are finished with this, we play percussion instruments from all over the world. I specialize in Afro-Cuban percussion and the children actually begin to learn the rhythmic language. For my older students I have a percussion workshop that meets once a month for an hour where we continue with our percussive training. Then I play guitar and we sing.

All in all this is a very creative program that introduces children to the musical language with many different instruments. It is a great deal of fun.

Space books up fast so please let me know if you are interested in the fall program. I will give you a tour of the studio and further information for the class. When kids go with their friends, it is really fun!

Sincerely,

Sheli

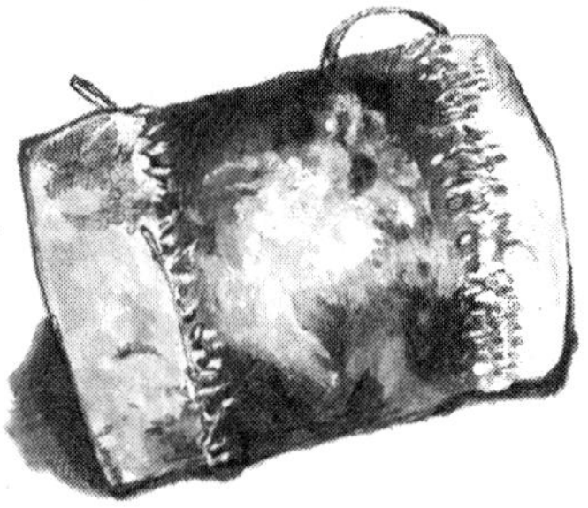

Student Gathering Points To Be Discussed With Parents

As I welcome parents and their children to The Music Studio for the semi-annual Student Gathering, I like to open the program with remarks about the Students' progress, and I like to present topics that I have discussed with my students or that are of immediate concern to we who are present.

1. Practice. Take the opportunity to speak to your parents about your expectations of the child's practice schedule. Don't forget to let them know that practice is an activity that gradually becomes more central to a person's life as he continues his music training.

2. Workshops. Report back to the parents on musical activity that has taken place at your studio. In my case, I speak about the percussion workshop, the harpsichord workshop, the meeting of baroqueniks, and the Junior Bach Festival.

3. Theory and Composition. If you have composers among you, take a moment to speak to the parents about the process of composition. If any of the children have written their pieces out, at any stage of complexity, please ask them to stand up and show their compositions to the group.

4. Be philosophical. The study of music is cultural, social, intellectual, and spiritual. We learn about ourselves by challenging ourselves in this difficult endeavor. Etc.

5. Acknowledge the parents. For example, this is what I recently said. "You are to be commended for your perseverance both as parents and students because there are a lot of distractions in today's world. It takes a degree of loyalty to make music a priority. A person does not become a good pianist by hoping to be one. There must be time to practice and absorb the material. It is a lifelong quest. That is why I ask ALL of you to carefully check how many programs you book your children into. I know that with Hebrew School it tends to get tight but I heartily suggest no more than three activities, at the most, and if one of those is religious school, when that ends, stay with two activities. Certainly you will give your children a chance to become better musicians.

Sample Pages From Student Notebooks

September 5

1-2-3-4-555
5-4-3-2-111

1-3-5-3-111
5-3-1-3-555

Rolling Song
Hands Alone and Hands Together
Hot Cross Buns with chords

November 10

C Major Scale
Right Hand 1-2-3-1-2-3-4-5
Left Hand 5-4-3-2-1-3-2-1
hands alone and hands together

C Major Arpeggio
Right Hand 1-2-3-5
Left Hand 5-4-2-1
hands alone and hands together

make music up

Twinkle Twinkle with one chord
Mary Had a Little lamb two chords
Chopsticks

Sample Pages From Student Notebooks

August 20

Major Scales
C-B, C#, Eb, F#

F# has f#, c#, g#, d#, a#, e#

R.H. 2-3-4-1-2-3-1-2
L.H. 4-3-2-1-3-2-1-2 1 octave

Major Arpeggios
C-B, C#, Eb
2 octaves

Czerny
#9 "llave" technique
#10 contrast between hands

Beethoven
Continue through Page 106

Purcell
Pg. 12 begin
Articulation at bars and at strong beat-quarter note downbeat

Sample Pages From Student Notebooks

April 25

Major Scales

C-C#-D-Eb-E-F-F#-G-Ab-A-Bb-B

Ab

R.H. 2-3-1-2-3-1-2-3
L.H. 3-2-1-4-3-2-1-2

Bb

R.H. 2-1-2-3-1-2-3-4
L.H. 3-2-1-4-3-2-1-2

I octave H.T.

Major Arpeggios

C-C#-D-Eb-E-F-F#-G-Ab-A-Bb-B

F#
On black notes
R.H. 1-2-3-1-2-3-5
L.H. 5-3-2-1-3-2-1

Arps beginning on finger 2 in both hands - C#, Eb, Ab, Bb

Czerny Review #1-#5

Kabalevsky, Pg. 3 begin Hands Alone

Turk, watch out for phrasing, think of articulation

Sample Pages From Student Notebooks

January 16

Major-minor Scales
1 oct. H.T.

Major-minor- Dominant 7th - dim minor Arps
3 octaves

Czerny
Pg. 30-31 #42

URTEXT
Mozart Sonatina in C

Bach - begin Pg. 36
R.H. only - with articulation

Chopin - practice w/o repeats
Good work! Focus

SAMPLE PAGES FROM STUDENT NOTEBOOKS

November 17

Major Scales
C-C#-D-Eb-E-F-F#-G-Ab-A-Bb-B

YES!! 2 octaves!!!!
Hurray!!!!!!!!!!!!!

Maj-min Arps
C-B 2 octaves chromatic

Theory Book Page 7

Your Score:

1. accidental signs go BEFORE the notes
2. put in I IV V signs where appropriate etc.
3. begin to think about time signatures as you write in the measure lines -
lightly - in pencil

Clementi
1st movement - notes
excellent phrasing

Bach
Great Articulation!
Begin the trio

Introduction To Percussion Patterns

Introduction to the percussion patterns of Master Drummer and Spiritual Leader Babatunde Olatunji from Nigeria. Babatunde Olatunji preaches love and peace through his musical message. He lives in New York with his band. He is the first person who introduced African drums to the United States.

1. **GN** - bottom sound
full hand touching mid drum
muffled or open sound
relaxed posture, arms in a smooth line

2.**GO** or **DO**
right hand plays **DO**
left hand plays **DO**
fingers closed playing ONLY with fingers at the edge of the drum

3. **PA** and **TA**
right hand plays **PA**
left hand plays **TA**
good posture, wrist moves up
padded edge of hand hits rim of drum and 4 fingers go down like "waving goodbye" then pop up again
just "tap" fingers to understand the beginning of the movement

GN GO DO GO
GN GN DO GO

This pattern is a Liberian peace song.

OLATUNJI'S DRUM EXERCISES

A	1	2	3	1	2	3	1	2	3	1	2	3
1.	GN		GO	DO			GN		GO	DO		
2.	GN		GO	DO	GO	DO	GN					
3.	GN		GO	DO	GO	DO	GN		GO	DO		
4.	GN		GO	DO	GO	DO	GN		PA			
5.	GN		GO	DO	GO	DO	GN		PA	TA		
6.	GN		GO	DO	GO	DO	GN	TA	GO	TA	GO	

B	1	2	3	4	1	2	3	4	1	2	3	4	1	2	3	4
1.	GN		DO		GN		DO		GN		DO		GO	DO		
2.	GN		PA	TA			PA	TA	GN		PA		GO	DO		
3.	GO	DO			GO	DO			GO	DO			GO	DO		

C	1	2	3	1	2	3	1	2	3	1	2	3
1. GO DO	PA		GN		GO	DO	PA				GO	DO
2. DO	PA		GN		GO	DO	PA		GO	DO		DO
3. GO DO	PA		PA	TA		TA	PA		GN		GO	DO

SOUNDS:	GUN (GN)	GO	DO	PA	TA
	BASS	OPEN TONE	OPEN TONE	SLAP	SLAP
	RIGHT HAND	RIGHT HAND	LEFT HAND	RIGHT HAND	LEFT HAND

GROUP LESSON PLANS

TUESDAY 3:00 - 3:30 JENNY, DON and BOBBY

At the piano: go over 1-2-3-4-555, 5-4-3-2-111, Hot Cross Buns, Twinkle Twinkle, and 1-3-5-3-111. If they can do 5-3-1-3-555 in the left hand that would be fine also. Each exercise can be done hands alone and handstogether. Each person takes turns. After this each person gets a chance to make something up. The others sit on the floor quietly while this person improvises. If someone goes on too long, you say, "wrap it up." Each person must listen to what he/she is doing and create an ending for their improvisation. Then we go to the instruments. First you take the Boomwhackers and go over beats with the kids. Start simple, 1-2-3-4 and vary it, such as 1-2-3 rest 1-2-3 rest 1-2- rest rest 1-2- rest rest 1 rest rest 4-1- rest rest 4-1 etc. Then see if they can do some more complex beats. You could try the clave beat. For the last 5 or 10 minutes they can do any instrument and be as loud as they want. You can discuss musical dynamics.

WEDNESDAY 4:00-5:00 JOHNNIE, ARTHUR AND STEVEN

Begin at the piano. These kids are more advanced. While you go over the material with one child, the others play quietly in the room. Sometimes they stay at the piano to listen to one another. The rules are that they must whisper if they are not at the piano and that they are not allowed to touch one another if they are playing quietly. Each boy has at least two pieces he is working on. When you finish this, they each have a chance to do their own improvisation. They are very talented. Just young. After the piano go to the instruments. Begin on the Boomwhackers. Go from easy to more difficult beats.

There are a number of Boomwhacker games that you can do together. Begin in a circle. Each person must hold a Boomwhacker in each hand. You begin by tapping a pattern on the Boomwhacker of the person next to you. If you begin with your right hand tap the pattern onto the left hand of the person next to you. He will in turn tap it with his other hand, his right hand, onto the Boomwhacker held in the left hand of the person next to him. This improves right left brain function. Go around in a circle and when the pattern is successfully returned to you, initiate a new pattern that is more complex. After this, they will play the drums. They also do "band". This is where they choose their instruments and then decide who will begin playing first. The first person begins then the others join in according to how loud their instruments are. The loudest instrument joins last. You should be playing also. We listen carefully to one another and try to make our beats either fit or correspond to the other beats. The object of this is that they are able to hear themselves as well as everybody else's instrument. Then at the end of class, the last 5 minutes, let them have some free time to make a splash. They can choose drums or any instrument and let them tell you what they would like to do. For instance, they may just want to play real loud. That is okay. Please join in. Part of the beauty of these lessons is that you the teacher get to play and improvise too. If I ever figure out something cool, like a good lick on the guitar or a rhythm that satisfies on one of the drums, I always stop the class and show them. This lets them know that I am listening to myself as well as to them and that I am being creative right there with them. This class knows the breathing technique. Use it if they need it.

GROUP CLASS THURSDAY 4:00-5:00 JERRY, KEVIN AND KENNY

These students know how to do scales and arpeggios. This is what we begin with. Scales one week, arpeggios the next. They tend to stay at the piano and watch each other. After technique, they go to their books. They usually have one or two pieces per book. After this they can do their improvisations for one another. They always have a lot to share and can always play pieces for each other that their parents taught them etc. They are smart and energetic. After solo time they go to the instruments. They are pretty sophisticated rhythmically. Begin with the Boomwhackers. Do not hesitate to tell them to breathe. They can get kind of clownish and I am sure they will try to test you. They must be gentle with the instruments. After Boomwhackers, please do some games. You can do a quiet band, where, following the same principles, each person needs to hear everyone else. Stagger when they come in and when they go out. Please always play as well. Choose your own instrument. Then the band can do musical dynamics. Lead them into a crescendo, then back down etc.

Talk about this and how it also relates to the piano.

GROUP CLASS THURSDAY 4:00-4:30 CARMEN AND SARAH

These girls are just beginning to learn to read. They are very sweet. They sit at the keyboard and you give them a piano lesson together. They may also request a story. Here is a story you can tell them. They will illustrate it with music. "Once upon a time there was a princess. She lived in a large castle made of gold. Her mother was the queen. One day the princess came down the stairs of her castle. There was a little kitten crying. She scooped up the little kitten and asked it why it was so sad. It was a magic kitten and it told her that it could not find its mother. She decided that she would help the little kitty. They wandered all through the golden palace. They looked into many different rooms. One room felt just like winter. When the princess opened the door everything was cold and snowy. Another room felt just like fall. When the princess opened the door everything was rainy and windy. Well, said the princess, I know your mother wouldn't be in there because cats don't like water! Meow, said the baby kitten. Finally they came to a warm cozy spot under the golden stairs. I think I recognize this, said the kitten. Sure enough, the mama kitten came out when she heard her baby's voice and was so happy to see her baby that she was licking her all over. After the princess had put the baby back she went to look for her own mother, the queen. Well, said the queen, here you are! You must be hungry for breakfast. And they went off arm in arm to eat."

When you tell this story, please pause at descriptive moments so that the children can play the feeling, or adjective, that you are at that moment describing. They can take turns as well as doing it at the same time. (e.g. Sarah play the kitten etc.) After this they can do their books for you. They generally have one or two pieces but like to review. Then they have their improvisational time at the keyboard. Finally, if there is time, they do instruments. On the instruments you can do lightweight rhythm training.

Student Photo Gallery

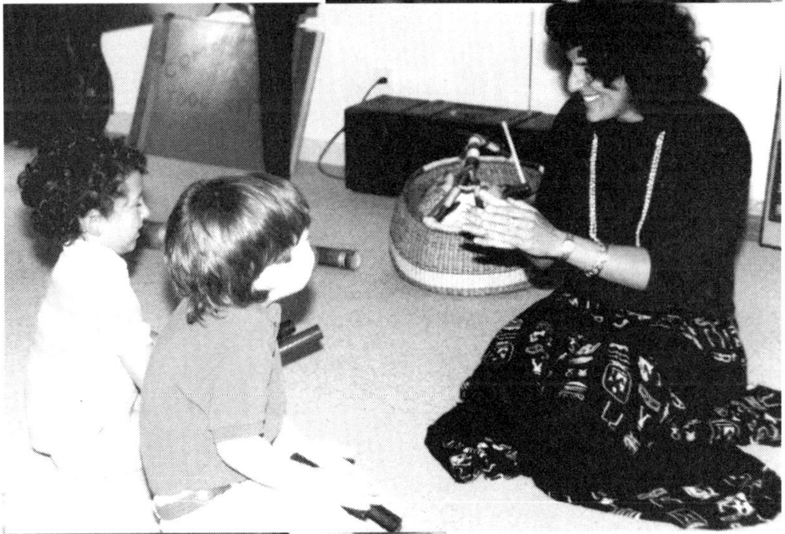

STUDENT PHOTO GALLERY

Student Photo Gallery

Story Ideas

All of these story themes can be woven into exciting stories for the children to improvise on. You should always look for a story that the children can illustrate with contrasting dynamics.

1. Adventure and Kindness

a. On the princess' birthday her mother the queen gives her a party and she gets to give gifts to all of her friends.
b. The princess is lonely and finds a friend, a magic rabbit, who can speak to her.
c. The pony and the princess go exploring and find an island that they must swim to. When they arrive they find an old Chinese palace.
d. The princess goes up the mountain to visit the witch on the top of the mountain.

2. Stories About Weather

a. Rainstorms with thunder
b. Light rain with the sun then coming out
c. Jumping into puddles
d. A windy sunny day

3. Verbs

a. Skipping and playing
b. Slowly walking
c. Crying and laughter
d. Climbing, running, being chased, hiding

4. Stories About Animals

a. Kitten stories. The kitten is lonely and afraid. There is a big dog living down the street. The dog chases the cat. She runs up a tree. The dog, barking frantically at the bottom of the tree, tries to climb the tree. The kitten cries, "Can't we just be friends?" The dog has never ever considered that possibility. She sits down to think. She decides it's a good idea. The cat comes down the tree and rides home on the big dog's back.

5. Magic Stories

a. The magic rock that turns kids into super kids. The homework is done in five minutes. A boy jumps out of his window and saves a girl's life. Then the rock is lost. The next person finds it. A new chapter for an ongoing story.

The possibilities are endless. Everyone loves sports stories, animal stories, adventure stories, stories about generosity and goodness. As you tell these stories the facility to make them up will increase. Use your imagination.

The stories work best when they have moral endings. Dogs and cats become friends. Girls and boys work together. Poor parents are given great handmade gifts by their children. Children prepare the Thanksgiving dinner for everyone. Sisters and brothers learn to cooperate.

These simple themes will enrich the student's knowledge of themselves and of the world through the musical experience.

Instrument List With Illustrations

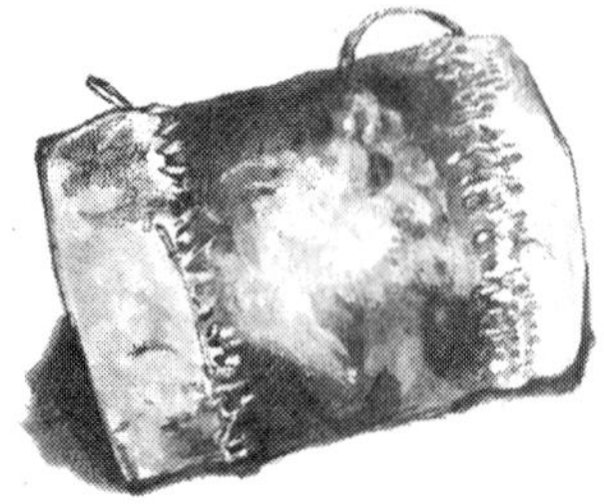

African drum

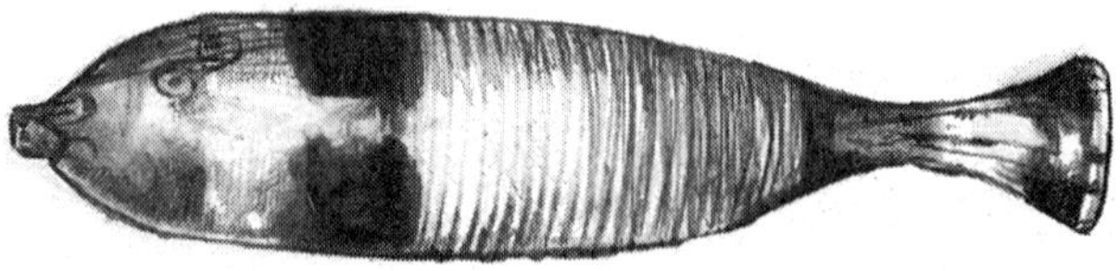

guiro

Boomwhacker Percussion Tubes

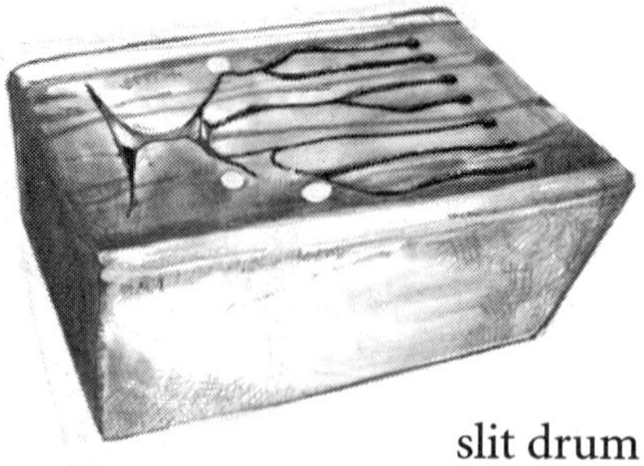

slit drum

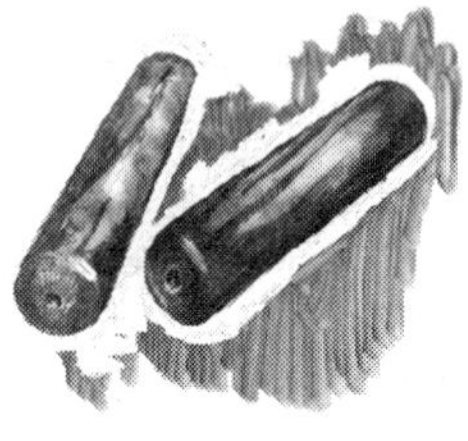

claves

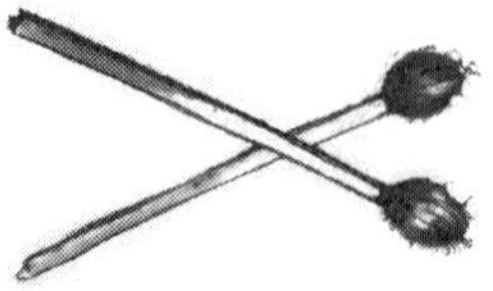

mallets

conga drum

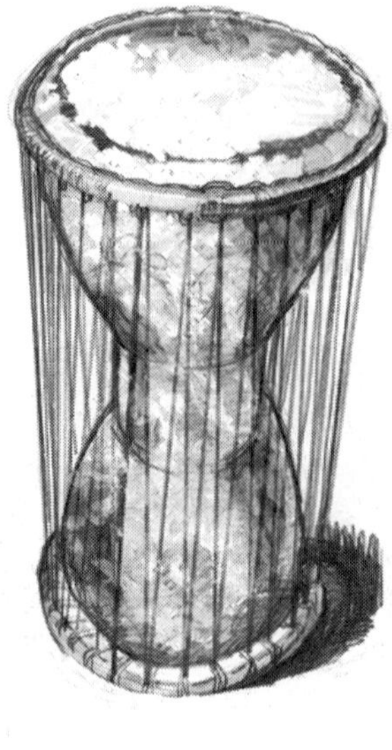

talking drum

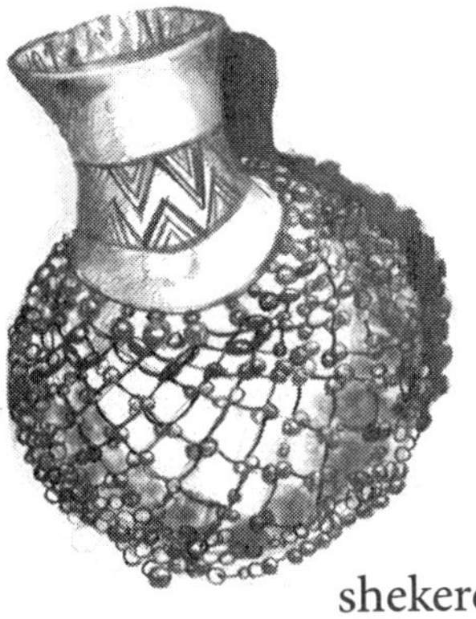

shekere

Remo drum head

rainstick

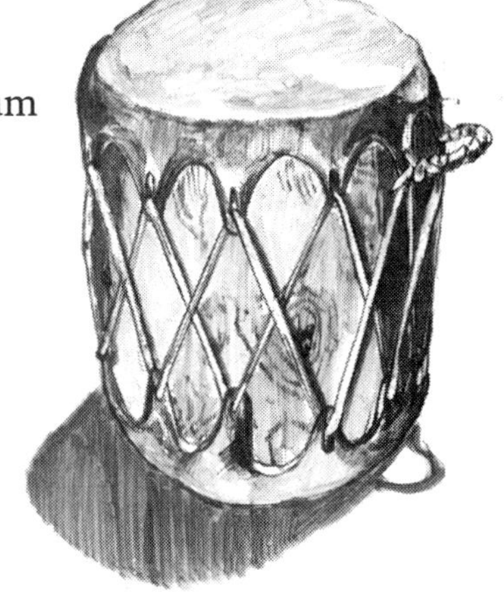

Native American drum

maracas

bongos

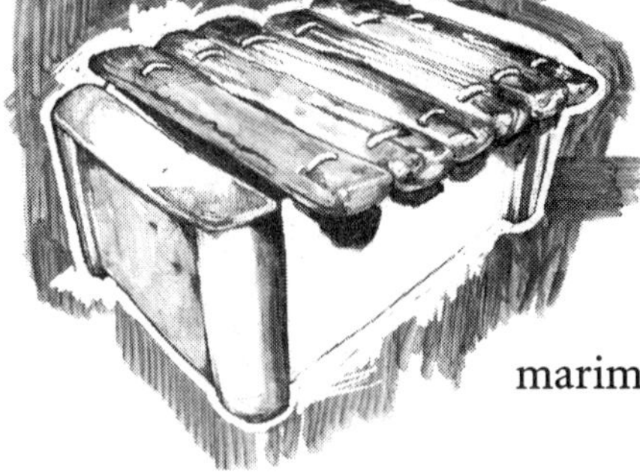

marimba

THE MAJOR SCALE CHART

Whole step whole step half step whole step whole step whole step half step.

C

RIGHT HAND 1-2-3-1-2-3-4-1-2-3-1-2-3-4-5
LEFT HAND 5-4-3-2-1-3-2-1-4-3-2-1-3-2-1

C#.....f# c# g# d# a# e# b#

R.H. 2-3-1-2-3-4-1-2-3-1-2-3-4-1-2
L.H. 3-2-1-4-3-2-1-3-2-1-4-3-2-1-2

D.....f# c#

same fingering as C

Eb.....bb eb ab

R.H. 2-1-2-3-4-1-2-3-1-2-3-4-1-2-3
L.H. 3-2-1-4-3-2-1-3-2-1-4-3-2-1-2

E.....f# c# g# d#

same fingering as C

F.....bb

R.H. 1-2-3-4-1-2-3-4-1-2-3-1-2-3-4
L.H. 5-4-3-2-1-3-2-1-4-3-2-1-3-2-1

F#.....f# c# g# d# a# e#

R.H. 2-3-4-1-2-3-1-2-3-4-1-2-3-1-2
L.H. 4-3-2-1-3-2-1-4-3-2-1-3-2-1-2

G.....f#

same fingering as C

Ab.....bb eb ab db

R.H. 2-3-1-2-3-1-2-3-4-1-2-3-1-2-3
L.H. 3-2-1-4-3-2-1-3-2-1-4-3-2-1-2

A.....f# c# g#

same fingering as C

Bb.....bb eb

R.H. 2-1-2-3-1-2-3-4-1-2-3-1-2-3-4
L.H. 3-2-1-4-3-2-1-3-2-1-4-3-2-1-2

B.....f# c# g# d# a#

R.H. 1-2-3-1-2-3-4-1-2-3-1-2-3-4-5
L.H. 4-3-2-1-4-3-2-1-3-2-1-4-3-2-1

The Harmonic Minor Scale Chart

Take the major scale and flat the 3rd note and flat the 6th note.

C

same fingering as C Major

C#

R.H. 2-3-1-2-3-1-2-3-4-1-2-3-1-2-3
L.H. 3-2-1-4-3-2-1-3-2-1-4-3-2-1-2

D

same fingering as D Major

Eb

R.H. 2-1-2-3-4-1-2-3-1-2-3-4-1-2-3
L.H. 2-1-4-3-2-1-3-2-1-4-3-2-1-3-2

F

same fingering as F Major

F#

R.H. 2-3-1-2-3-1-2-3-4-1-2-3-1-2-3
L.H. 4-3-2-1-3-2-1-4-3-2-1-3-2-1-2

G

same fingering as G Major

Ab

same fingering as Ab Major

A

same fingering as A Major

Bb

R.H. 2-1-2-3-1-2-3-4-1-2-3-1-2-3-4
L.H. 2-1-3-2-1-4-3-2-1-3-2-1-4-3-2

B

same fingering as B Major

The Melodic Minor Scale Chart

flat the 3rd on the way up and flat the 3rd the 6th and the 7th on the way down

C

same fingering as C Major

C#

UP

R.H. 2-3-1-2-3-4-1-2-3-1-2-3-4-1-3

L.H. 3-2-1-4-3-2-1-3-2-1-4-3-2-1-2

DOWN

R.H. 3-2-1-4-3-2-1-3-2-1-4-3-2-1-2

L.H. 2-1-2-3-4-1-2-3-1-2-3-4-1-2-3

D

same fingering as D Major

Eb

UP& DOWN

R.H. 2-1-2-3-4-1-2-3-1-2-3-4-1-2-3

L.H.2-1-4-3-2-1-3-2-1-4-3-2-1-3-2

E

same fingering as E Major

F

same fingering as F Major

F#

UP & DOWN

R.H. 2-3-1-2-3-4-1-2-3-1-2-3-4-1-2

L.H. 4-3-2-1-3-2-1-4-3-2-1-3-2-1-2

(continued)

G

same as G Major

Ab

UP

R.H. 2-3-1-2-3-1-2-3-4-1-2-3-1-2-3

L.H. 3-2-1-4-3-2-1-3-2-1-4-3-2-1-2

DOWN

R.H. 3-2-1-3-2-1-4-3-2-1-3-2-1-3-2

L.H. 2-3-1-2-3-1-2-3-4-1-2-3-1-2-3

A

same as A Major

Bb

UP

R.H. 2-1-2-3-1-2-3-4-1-2-3-1-2-3-4

L.H. 3-2-1-4-3-2-1-3-2-1-4-3-2-1-2

DOWN

R.H. 4-3-2-1-3-2-1-4-3-2-1-3-2-1-2

L.H. 2-3-4-1-2-3-1-2-3-4-1-2-3-1-2

B

same as B Major

THE MAJOR AND MINOR ARPEGGIO CHARTS

MAJORS

C-D-E-F-G-A

R.H. 1-2-3-1-2-3-5

L.H. 5-4-2-1-4-2-1

B

R.H. 1-2-3-1-2-3-5

L.H. 5-3-2-1-3-2-1

C#- Eb- Ab- Bb

R.H. 2-1-2-4-1-2-4

L.H. 2-1-4-2-1-4-2

F#

R.H. 1-2-3-1-2-3-5

L.H. 5-3-2-1-3-2-1

MINORS: flat the 3rd

C- D- E- F- G- A- B- C#- Ab

same fingering as Majors

Eb

R.H. 1-2-3-1-2-3-5

L.H. 5-4-2-1-4-2-1

F#

R.H. 2-1-2-4-1-2-4

L.H. 2-1-4-2-1-4-2

Bb

R.H. 2-3-1-2-3-1-2

L.H. 3-2-1-3-2-1-2

THE DOMINANT 7TH AND DIMINISHED ARPEGGIO CHARTS

DOMINANT 7ths: add the major 7th and flat it

C- D- E- F- G- A- B

R.H. 1-2-3-4-1-2-3-4-5

L.H. 5-4-3-2-1-4-3-2-1

C#- Eb- Ab- Bb

R.H. 2-1-2-3-4-1-2-3-4

L.H. 2-1-4-3-2-1-4-3-2

F#

R.H. 2-3-4-1-2-3-4-1-2

L.H. 4-3-2-1-4-3-2-1-2

DIMINISHED: flat the 3rd and the 5th and add the 6th

C- D- E- F- G- A- B

R.H. 1-2-3-4-1-2-3-4-5

L.H. 5-4-3-2-1-4-3-2-1

C#

R.H. 2-1-2-3-4-1-2-3-4

L.H. 2-1-4-3-2-1-4-3-2

Eb

R.H. 2-3-1-2-3-4-1-2-3

L.H. 4-3-2-1-4-3-2-1-2

F#

R.H. 2-3-4-1-2-3-4-1-2

L.H. 2-1-4-3-2-1-4-3-2

Ab

R.H.2-1-2-3-4-1-2-3-4

L.H. 2-1-4-3-2-1-4-3-2

Bb

R.H. 2-3-1-2-3-4-1-2-3

L.H. 4-3-2-1-4-3-2-1-2

CIRCLE OF FIFTHS

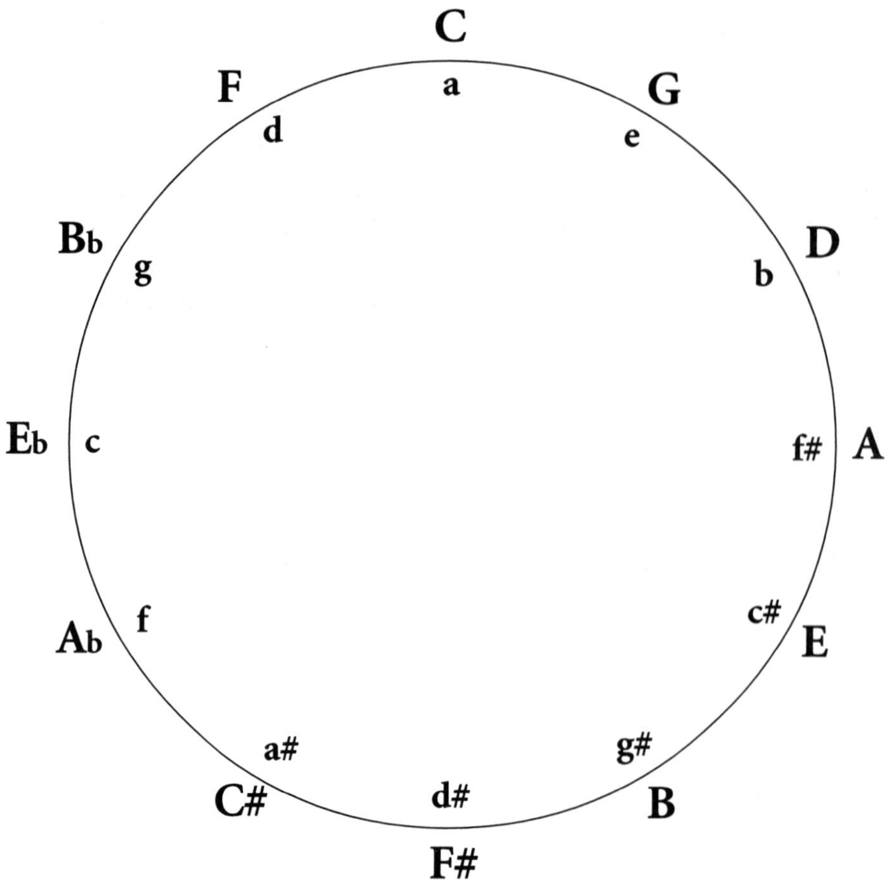

The keys outside the circle are the Major keys. The keys within the circle are the relative minor keys (three half steps down from the Major). Read the circle clockwise. All of the keys are spaced at an interval of a fifth.

RECOMMENDED EDITIONS

There are certain prerequisites that go into choosing an edition. The first quality that is examined is if the edition is urtext. This means that the edition has come to us with as little editorial input as possible. (This is not applicable to method books.) When we are choosing an edition that is edited, we want to know the reputation of the editor. If we are satisfied with the editorial input, which can range from phrasing to dynamics of all sorts, then we can buy with confidence.

An edition should be easy to read, with clear print. There are many variations of paper, shade, and print so be sure to examine various editions of the same work carefully. You will begin to learn about what you like and what you don't like.

When choosing editions for your students, take into account the students' age. This may affect the size of the type (as well as other considerations) you will choose.

Here is a partial list of the Editions that are currently in use at my studio:

For Adult Beginners:

The University Piano Series Book 1, Hershal Pyle,
 Campus Publication, Bradenton, Florida
Microcosmos Volumes 1 & 2, Bela Bartok, Boosey and Hawkes
Czerny-Schaum, Book 1

For Children:

Teaching Little Fingers to Play, John Thompson
Pre-A Piano Course, John W. Schaum
Music Lessons Have Begun, Leila Fletcher

To Continue:

The First Grade Book, John Thompson's Modern Course for the Piano
Piano Course Book 2, Maxwell Eckstein
Piano Course Lessons Grade 1, Michael Aarons
Czerny Schaum Book 1&2
Michael Aarons Piano Course Theory Books 1-6
Celebration Series Book 1, Frederick Harris Music
Suzuki Piano School Volumes 1-3
Beethoven, 16 of his Easiest Piano Selections, Alfred
Klavierstucke Piano Pieces, Konemann Music Budapest
Klavierwerke (Auswahel), Henle
Khatchaturian, Album for Young People, Alfred
Shostakovich, 6 pieces for Children, Alfred
Kabalevsky, Anson Introduces Books 1-2, Willis Music
Kabalevsky, First Book for Pianists, Alfred or Kalmus

Bach: G. Henle Verlag Urtext Editions:

1. Notebook from Anna Magdalena Bach
2. Small Preludes and Fugues
3. Inventions and Sinfonien
4. French Suites
5. English Suites
6. Goldberg Variations
7. Six Partitas

Dover Editions:

1. Miscellaneous Keyboard works; Toccatas, Fugues and other Pieces
2. Well Tempered Clavier Book 1 & 2
3. Complete Concertos for 2 or more Harpsichords

Other Editions:

1. J.S. Bach Open Score The Well Tempered Clavier Books 1 & 2, The 48 Fugues and 4 Preludes, Medallion Guild, Laurette Goldberg, Editor
2. Well Tempered Clavier Book 1 & 2, Associated Board, Richard Jones, Editor
3. Notenbuchlein Fur Anna Magdalena Bach, Schott
4. Englische Suiten & Franzosische Suiten, Konemann Music Budapest
5. Well Tempered Clavier Books I & II, Baerenreiter
6. Clavierubung I & II, Baerenreiter
7. Well Tempered Clavier Book I, Alfred (reference)
8. The Well Tempered Clavier of J.S. Bach, A Handbook for Keyboard Teachers and Performers. By Laurette Goldberg, Music Sources

Early Music Dover Editions:

1. The Fitzwilliam Virginal Book
2. My Ladye Nevells Booke
3. Purcell, The Complete Keyboard
4. Rameau, The Complete Works for Solo Keyboard
5. Couperin, Complete Keyboard Works and Miscellaneous pieces

Other Early Music Editions:

1. Scarlatti, Essercizi 30 Sonatas for the Keyboard, Schirmer, Fernando Valenti, Editor
2. Scarlatti, 60 Sonatas, Schirmer, 2 volumes, Ralph Kirkpatrick, Editor
3. Scarlatti, Anson Introduces, Willis Music
4. Couperin, L'Art de Toucher Le Clavecin, Breitkopf & Hartel
5. Haydn, Keyboard Sonatas Band 1 & 2, Henle
6. Haydn, Klaviersonaten Vol I-III, Carisch
7. Handel, Keyboard Sonatas, Dover
8. Beethoven, Klaviersonaton Vol I, Weiner Urtext

9. Beethoven, Variations Volume 1, Wiener Urtext
10. Bach, Wilhelm Friedemann, Notebook for, Baraenreiter & Weiner Urtext
11. The Vienna Urtext Guide to Piano Literature, Compiled & Introduced by Maurice Hinson (reference)
12. Domenico Scarlatti Thematic Index according to Ralph Kirkpatrick and Emilia Fadini, by Laurette Goldberg, Music Sources (reference)

Henle Editions of Mozart:

Klavierstucke
Klaviersonaten Band 1 & 2
Viennese Sonatinas (originally for Bassett Horns)

Other Mozart Editions:

Variations for Klavier, Wiener Urtext
Piano Concertos in full score, Dover

Beethoven Henle and Dover Editions:

Klavierstucke
Klaviersonaten Band 1 & 2

Czerny:

Czerny Germer Book 1 & 2, Boston Music or Alfred Edition
Opus 849, Schirmer
Opus 299, Schirmer

Chopin:

Waltzes, Schirmer, Joseffy, Editor
Etudes, Paderewski
Preludes, Paderewski
Ballades, Paderewski
Impromptus, Paderewski
Lemoine Editions

GLOSSARY

ACCENT	point of emphasis
ACCIDENTALS	sharps, flats, naturals etc. other than in key signatures
ALLEMANDE	German dance
ARPEGGIO	tones of a chord played one note at a time
ARTICULATION	distinctness of execution, space between the notes
BARCAROLE	Venetian gondolier's song in 6/8 or 12/8 time
BAROQUE	musical style personified by Bach and Handel etc. 1570-1790
BASS CLEF	F clef on the fourth line, in piano left hand
BOLERO	Spanish dance in 3/4 time
BOUREE	French dance in duple time
BRAVURA	boldness and dash
CADENCE	ending of a phrase or section
CANON	round
CANTABILE	in singing style
CHICANO	stately variations on a ground bass in 3/4 time
CHORD	combination of two or more tones
CHROMATIC	by half steps
CODA	ending section
COMMON TIME	4/4 time
CONCERTO	piece for soloist with orchestral accompaniment
COUNTERPOINT	two or more musical lines at the same time
COURANTE	French dance in 3/2 time
CRESCENDO	grow gradually louder
CUT TIME	2/2 time
DIMINUENDO	grow gradually softer
DOLCE	sweet

DOT	over a note: articulate shorter than full value. to the right of a note: add half of its time value to value of note
DOUBLE BAR	two vertical lines at end of section or piece
DYNAMICS	expression, different degrees of power applied to notes, signs words and phrases given to the performer to clarify the composer's intentions
ETUDE	exercise or study piece
FANTASIE	music in which a composer yields to his imagination and gives free scope to his ideas without restrictions in form
FORTEPIANO	the principle of striking the hammers for this precursor to the modern piano was invented by Cristofori in Padua Italy in 1710. great improvements were made and by the turn of the century (19th) the piano was functionable
FARANDOLE	rapid circle dance in 6/8 time
FIRST ENDING	to be played the first time but not on second of a repeated section
FORTE	loud
FORTEPIANO	precursor to the modern piano
FORTISSIMO	very loud
FUGUE	highest form of imitative counterpoint, a composition in strict style in which a subject is proposed by one part and answered by other parts according to certain rules, a contrapuntal development of the subject which is announced and quite alone at the begin ning, most fugues develop an exposition made up of a subject, which is a figure not a melody, an answer which is often the subject reproduced in the dominant and a counter-subject, which is a contrasted phrase accompanying the subject or answer at the entrance of the second voice
GIGUE	French version of a jig
HABANERA	Cuban dance in duple time
HARMONY	combination of tones, art of combining sounds into chords
HARPSICHORD	is controlled through a plucking device, similar to fingernails, and functions somewhat like a large mechanized guitar, is older than the clavichord, but not as loud as an organ, is portable and can be easily heard in a large room, has no absolute dynamic gradation, although color change through registration is possible on many harpsichords, ie engaging additional layers of strings, dynamics are created through articulation, touch and rhythmic alteration, two notes are twice as loud as one etc, chords and rapid figurated passages are intended to be louder on harpsichord, clarity and texture are the expressive tools, each part written for the harpsichord is completely delineated, a clear and lively tone is produced, the strings are stretched over two strips of wood called the bridge and the nut, the bridge is glued to a thin sheet of wood called the soundboard, the nut is glued to a block of wood that runs parallel to the keyboards and holds the tuning pins, when a string is plucked, its vibrations are transmitted by the bridge to the soundboard,

	which then transmits the vibrations to the sides and bottom of the instrument, called the case, and then into the air, usually two or three strings are plucked, most harpsichords have two or three strips of wood called registers that are used to move the sets of jacks into or out of contact with their sets of strings one set of strings sounds an octave higher than the other and can be used to add to the sound, the instrument first appeared in the 1300's by the late 1500's the instrument had become popular, during the 1600's Italian and Flemish draftsmen built simple harpsichords, by the turn of the century they became more elaborate, had two manuals plus a third set of strings, and were painted extravagantly
IMPRESSIONISM	musical style personified by Debussy and Ravel
IMPROVISATION	composing music as it is being performed
INTERPRETATION	way of expressing the meaning of the music
JACK	the quill which strikes the strings of a harpsichord
JAM	improvise
KEYBOARD	the rows of keys upon a harpsichord, fortepiano, organ, piano etc. the oldest actually existing keyboard of present style is on a spinet in the Paris Conservatiore dated 1523.
KEYNOTE	root note of the key
LARGO	slowest tempo mark
LEGATO	smooth and connected
LEGER LINE	extra line to extend the staff
LEGGIERO	light and airy
MALAGUENA	Spanish folk music from Malaga
MARCATO	distinctly marked
MAZURKA	Polish dance in 3/4 with variable accent on the third beat
MELODY	tune
MENO MOSSO	less rapid
METER	meter is the rhythm of the phrase, not of the measure
METRONOME	invented in 1815 by John Maelzel in Germany for measuring time or duration of notes, a pendulum which can be shortened or lengthened, with a movable counterweight which swings to and fro and clicks, there are electronic metronomes, Beethoven and Czerny were the first composers to use
MEZZOFORTE	medium loud
MEZZOPIANO	medium soft

MINOR SCALE	harmonic and melodic, in the first the half-steps falls between the second and the third, fifth and sixth, and seventh and eighth degrees, both ascending and descending, in the melodic, the half-step falls between the second and the third and seventh and eighth degrees ascending, and between the sixth and fifth, and third and second, descending
MINUET	early French dance in 3/4 time
MODERATOR	moderate speed
MORDENT	rapidly moving from main note to neighboring auxiliary note, accenting the primary note
MUSICALITY	natural artistry in performance
MUSICIANSHIP	skill and knowledge in the art of music
NOCTURNE	dreamy, sentimental piece
OCTAVE	interval measuring eight diatonic(scale) degrees
PARALLEL MOTION	two or more musical lines moving in the same direction
PUI MOSSO	more rapid
PASSACAGLIA	stately variations in 3/4 over a ground bass
PAVAN	stately slow dance in 2/2
PERCUSSION	to strike to create a sound, general name for percussion instruments, drums cymbals etc.
PHRASING	dividing the musical sentences into rhythmical sections
PIANISSIMO	very soft
PIANO	soft
POLONAISE	Polish dance in moderate 3/4 time
PRELUDE	musical introduction
PRESTO	very rapid
PROGRAM MUSIC	music describing specific scenes or events
RALLENTANDO	grow slowly gradually
RHYTHM	length and accentuation of tones or groups
RITARDANDO	slow down gradually
ROMANTIC	musical style personified by Schumann, Chopin etc.
SCALE	stepwise progression of tones

SFORZANDO	sudden marked emphasis
SHARP	# sign raising the note the pitch of one tone, a chromatic half-step
SIGNATURE	the sharps flats or numbers in fractional form given at the beginning of the compositions, the former, key signatures, and the latter, time signatures
SLUR	curved line to indicate connection
SONATA	piece in three or four movements for one or two instruments
SONATINA	small sonata
SPINET	popular from the 1500's through the 1700's, looking like a miniature grand piano, operates like a harpsichord though the sound is not as rich, wire strings are plucked by quills or pieces of leather
STACCATO	separated abruptly
STAFF	the notes are written on the five horizontal and parallel lines
SYNCOPATION	displacement of usual emphasis on strong beats, hides the beats in tied over notes
TECHNIQUE	skill and proficiency
TEMPO	Italian word for time, the speed of rhythm, the rapidity with which natural accents follow one another
TEMPO RUBATO	robbed or stolen time
TIME SIGNATURE	indicator of meter
TONE	sound of recognizable pitch
TONALITY	placement of tones in relation to key
TRANSCRIPTION	rewritten for another instrument or voice
TRANSPOSITION	rewritten in another key
TREBLE CLEF	G clef on the second line, right hand
TRILL	rapid alternation between two neighboring tones
TURN	four grace notes: upper neighbor, main note, lower neighbor, main note
VIVACE	lively and animated
VIRGINAL	keyboard instrument popular during the 1500's, resembling a harpsichord, with a rectangular case, the keyboard being on one of the longer sides, the pressed keys producing a light clear tone from small pieces of quill or leather that pluck the metal strings
WALTZ	dance in 3/4 time

BIBLIOGRAPHY

1. Carl Czerny
On the Proper Performance of all Beethoven's Works For The Piano
Edited and with a Commentary by Paul Badura-Skoda
Universal Edition U.S.A. 1970

2. Francois Couperin
L'ART de Toucher Le Clavecin
The Art of Playing the Harpsichord 1717
Edited by Anna Linde
Breitkopf & Hartel - Wiesbaden 1933

3. Africa O-Ye!
A Celebration of African Music
by Graeme Ewens
Sango Publications, London 1991

4. The Well Tempered Clavier of J.S. Bach
A Handbook for Keyboard Teachers and Performers
by Laurette Goldberg
Music Sources, Center for Historically Informed Performances, Inc. 1995

5. John Christian Bach Mozart's Friend and Mentor
by Heinz Gartner
Amadeus Press 1989

6. Elson's Pocket Music Dictionary
Oliver Ditson Company
Theodore Presser Company 1909

7. The World Book Encyclopedia
World Book, Inc. 1990

NOTES

NOTES

RHYTHMTWISTERS RECORDS ANNOUNCES:

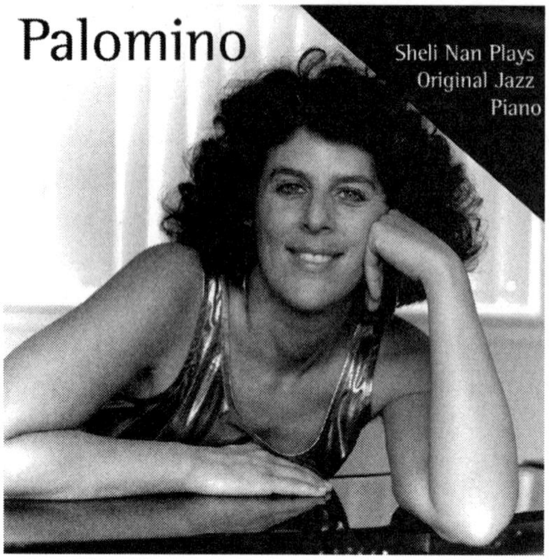

PALOMINO
Sheli Nan Plays Original Jazz Piano
Sheli's signature album of original jazz and Latin piano.

"An energetic lady who knows her way around a keyboard...a bit of Latin, a touch of swing, a complex pattern and a display of Nan's superb technique."
Phil Elwood

OLD AGE MEETS NEW AGE
Sheli Nan at the Harpsichord

"It's no news that over the last few decades, New Age music has proliferated. Has anyone, though, used the harpsichord to send that particular message? An instrument from centuries of yore, imaginatively adapted to the styles and colors of today's improvisatory thinking - that is what Sheli Nan has done, even throwing in a few old timers, such as Baroquists Telemann and Frescobaldi, and for good measure creating a bluesy Bach boogie. Meet the harpsichord on new ground in this definitely fun disc.
Igor Kipnis

UNDERCURRENTS
by The Elixirs

"Wacky performance art and a clever sense of humor create a musical experience that is hard to forget. Ms. Nan's musicians, like figments of a fractured personality, play music that comes from dreams and a parallel universe. This CD, only for the adventurous and open minded, is a trip into inner space. As the liner notes say, 'sound = motivation, ideas = catalyst, music = elixir, sound + ideas =music, music =undercurrents. Some of the instruments featured on this disc are keyboards, marimba, vocals, drums, percussion, bass, flute and horns."
ELISHA

To order any of the above CDs or to order more copies of The Essential Piano Teacher's Guide, please contact: RHYTHMTWISTERS, P.O. Box 5173, Berkeley, California 94705, or use the order form below.
For more information e-mail: Themuse23@aol.com or visit the website: www.shelinan.com

For THE ESSENTIAL PIANO TEACHER'S GUIDE book orders:
_____ (quantity requested)

Send check or money order for$19.95 + 8.25% sales tax (within California) + $4.00 shipping and handling to RHYTHMTWISTERS
P.O. Box 5713
Berkeley, CA 94705

For CD orders, send check or money order for $19.95 + 8.25% sales tax (within California) + $4.00 shipping and handling to the above address. Specifiy quantity requested.
_____ PALOMINO Sheli Nan Plays Original Jazz Piano
_____ OLD AGE MEETS NEW AGE Sheli Nan at the Harpsichord
_____ UNDERCURRENTS by The Elixirs

Your name: ____________________
Address: ____________________
Contact phone or e.mail address: ____________________